BERLIN *MADE EASY* ✤

Andy Herbach

Author of *Paris Made Easy, Provence Made Easy,
Amsterdam Made Easy,* and co-author of the
Eating & Drinking on the Open Road guides

Open Road Publishing

Open Road Publishing

We offer travel guides to American and foreign locales. Our books tell it like it is, often with an opinionated edge, and our experienced authors always give you all the information you need to have the trip of a lifetime. Write for your free catalog of all our titles.

Open Road Publishing
P.O. Box 284, Cold Spring Harbor, NY 11724
E-mail: Jopenroad@aol.com

Acknowledgments
English editors: Jonathan Stein and Marian Olson
German editor: Professor Robert Jamison
Maps from designmaps.com
Website (www.eatndrink.com): McDill Design and
Susan Chwae
Contributor: Karl Raaum
Additional research: Mark Berry, Jeff Kurz, Jim Mortell and
Dan Schmidt

ABOUT THE AUTHOR

Andy Herbach is the author of Open Road Publishing's *Paris Made Easy*, *Provence Made Easy*, *Amsterdam Made Easy*, and is the co-author of Open Road's *Eating & Drinking in Paris*, *Eating & Drinking in Italy*, *Eating & Drinking in Spain*, and *Eating & Drinking in Latin America*. Look for his forthcoming *Europe Made Easy*. E-mail Andy corrections, additions, and comments at eatndrink@aol.com or through his website at www.eatndrink.com.

TABLE OF CONTENTS

Introduction　7

1. Sights　8
Top Ten Sights　8
Mitte (City Center)　10
Museumsinsel (Museum Island)　23
Alexanderplatz　27
Nikolaiviertel (Nicholas Quarter)　30
Scheunenviertel　32
Prenzlauer Berg　37
Friedrichshain　40
Potsdamer Platz　43
Tiergarten　49
Schöneberg/Kreuzberg　54
Kurfürstendamm　60
Charlottenburg　65
Off the Beaten Path　69
Excursions　73

2. Walks　79
Berlin Wall Walking Tour　79
Gendarmenmarkt Walking Tour　84
East Berlin Walking Tour　88
West Berlin Walking Tour　94
Charlottenburg Walking Tour　100

3. Miscellany　104
Dining　104
Airports & Getting Around　108
Berlin by Season　111

Other Basic Information   112
Hotels   117
Helpful Phrases   118

Index   121

MAPS

Germany   6
Berlin   9
City Center: North   12
City Center: South   18
Alexanderplatz/Nikolaiviertel   27
Scheunenviertel   33
Prenzlauer Berg   38
Friedrichshain   41
Potsdamer Platz/Kulturforum   44
Tiergarten   50
Schöneberg/Kreuzberg   55
Kurfürstendamm   61
Charlottenburg   66
Berlin Wall Walking Tour   80
Gendarmenmarkt Walking Tour   85
East Berlin Walking Tour   89
West Berlin Walking Tour   96-97
Charlottenburg Walking Tour   101

INTRODUCTION

Berlin is forever evolving. Even if you visited just a short time ago, you can be sure the city will always have something new to offer.

Berlin is truly like no other city in the world. Despite the ravages of war, the brutal division of the wall and the struggles of reunification, Berlin continues to look forward.

You can marvel at historic buildings painstakingly renovated (such as the impressive Reichstag), or experience some of the most innovative modern architecture anywhere (and, particularly at Alexanderplatz in former East Berlin, some of the worst). But Berlin isn't about buildings. It's about feeling alive and vibrant.

There's something for everyone. From museums like the Pergamonmuseum, with some of the world's greatest masterpieces, to poignant memorials like the Memorial to the Murdered Jews, to an exciting nightlife unlike any other city in Europe, Berlin will not disappoint.

As our title says, this little guide will make your trip to Berlin easy. Tuck it into your pocket and head out for a great day of sightseeing: You'll have over 100 places of interest at your fingertips, with insider tips on cafés, restaurants, and shops. We've also given directions for sight-filled walks around the city, including around both former East and West Berlin, along the former Berlin Wall, and to the museums in Charlottenburg.

Forget those large, bulky travel tomes. This handy little pocket guide to Berlin is all you need to make your visit enjoyable, memorable—*and easy.*

1. SIGHTS

TOP SIGHTS

1. Reichstag
The German parliament building with its fabulous modern dome.

2. Brandenburger Tor
The Brandenburg Gate, the gateway to **Unter den Linden**, East Berlin's main street.

3. Haus am Checkpoint Charlie
The story of a city divided.

4. Kurfürstendamm
West Berlin's main street has great shopping, and the **Kaiser-Wilhelm-Gedächtniskirche** (Kaiser Wilhelm Memorial Church).

5. Tiergarten
Berlin's huge green space in the center of the city is home to the **Zoologischer Garten Berlin** (Berlin Zoo), **Siegessäule** (Victory Column), and **Schloss Bellevue** (the home of Germany's president).

6. Gendarmenmarkt
One of Europe's most beautiful squares.

7. Museumsinsel
An island in the middle of the Spree River that's home to the **Pergamonmuseum**.

8. Potsdamer Platz
Innovative modern architecture and the **Kulturforum**, home to some of the world's greatest art treasures.

9. Denkmal für die Ermordeten Juden Europas
The Memorial to the Murdered European Jews recalls the unimaginable.

10. Alexanderplatz
East Berlin's huge square, dominated by the television tower.

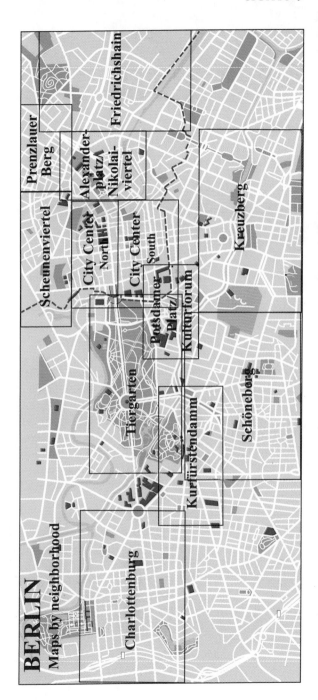

BERLIN
Maps by neighborhood

Charlottenburg

Prenzlauer Berg

Friedrichshain

Scheunenviertel

Alexander-platz/Nikolai-viertel

City Center North

City Center South

Potsdamer Platz

Kulturforum

Kreuzberg

Tiergarten

Kurfürstendamm

Schöneberg

Mitte (City Center)

Brandenburger Tor
(Brandenburg Gate)
Western end of Unter den Linden
Admission: Free
S-Bahn: Unter den Linden

Probably Berlin's most recognizable sight. This famous gate was originally called the "Gate of Peace" ("Friedenstor"). Built in 1791 as a triumphal arch, it was one of 18 gates in the capital of Prussia. The gate features six Doric columns topped by the Goddess of Victory driving a four-horse chariot (the **Quadriga**). Napoleon removed it when he conquered Berlin in 1806. The current statue is a copy dating back to 1958. The gate has been the center of German history for two centuries and the backdrop of many Nazi propaganda films. Badly damaged during World War II, for years it was in a sort of no man's land as part of East Berlin. When the wall came down, it was the center of huge celebrations. The gate once symbolized a divided city. Now it's again a symbol of a united and peaceful Germany. At night, the gate is beautifully illuminated.

Raum der Stille
(Room of Silence)
North wing of the Brandenburg Gate
Tel. 3059583
Open daily 10am-6pm with extended hours Apr-Oct
S-Bahn: Unter den Linden

Visitors can sit quietly in a small room built into the guard station in the northern wing of the Brandenburg Gate. It's dedicated to contemplating Berlin's history and praying for world peace. This sanctuary is modeled after a similar room at the United Nations in New York City.

Tourist-Information Center
South wing of the Brandenburg Gate
Open daily 10am-6pm with extended hours Apr-Oct
S-Bahn: Unter den Linden
www.btm.de

Brochures and maps will help you navigate the city and alert you to new attractions and current events throughout Berlin. The staff speaks English. The detailed map of Berlin sold here costs less than €1.

Unter den Linden
The street running east to west from the Brandenburg Gate to Museumsinsel
S-Bahn: Unter den Linden

This famous street got its name from the thousands of linden trees that line it. In the 18th and 19th centuries, the street was lined with beautiful buildings. In the 1920s, this was one of Europe's grandest boulevards. Hitler wanted to replace the trees with Nazi flags, a plan that was strongly opposed. Although most of the buildings were destroyed in World War II, many have been restored. When I visited this street in the mid-1980s when it was part of East Berlin, it was depressing. Today, it's vibrant and a great place to stroll. You can take a walk down this street in the East Berlin Walking Tour later in this book.

Pariser Platz
East of the Brandenburg Gate (the square facing the Brandenburg Gate)
S-Bahn: Unter den Linden

The name of this square "celebrates" the German occupation of Paris in 1814. This was ground zero for bombing by the Allies in World War II. Today, it's lined with banks, hotels, German governmental offices and embassies, including, ironically, the French Embassy. You'll also find the British Embassy at 70 Wilhelmstrasse (just around the corner from the square) and the U.S. Embassy, to open in the southern corner of the square. The very fancy Adlon Hotel is also here. Its guests have included Greta Garbo and Michael Jackson. (Remember when "the Gloved One" dangled his baby from the window? That was at the Adlon.)

Restaurant Tip:
Lorenz Adlon
77 Unter den Linden (in the Adlon Hotel)
Tel. 22611906
Closed Sun and Mon and mid-Jul to mid-Aug
S-Bahn: Unter den Linden

This elegant restaurant serves French, German and Alsatian food. Excellent service and extraordinary prices to go along with the extraordinary views of Pariser Platz and the Brandenburg Gate. Very Expensive.

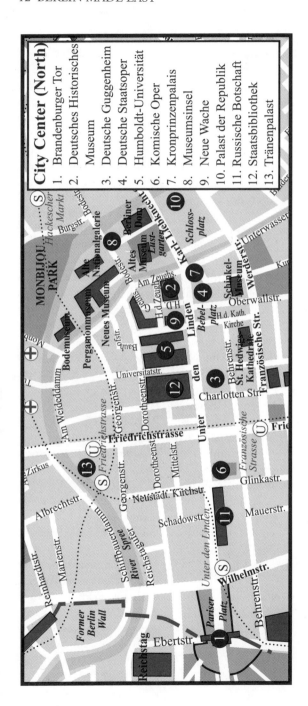

City Center (North)

1. Brandenburger Tor
2. Deutsches Historisches Museum
3. Deutsche Guggenheim
4. Deutsche Staatsoper
5. Humboldt-Universität
6. Komische Oper
7. Kronprinzenpalais
8. Museumsinsel
9. Neue Wache
10. Palast der Republik
11. Russische Botschaft
12. Staatsbibliothek
13. Tränenpalast

ABBREVIATIONS

• When you see this symbol, ß, it means "ss." So, the street Friedrichstrasse looks like "Friedrichstraße."

• You'll see the abbreviation GDR used in this book. GDR is short for German Democratic Republic, the name of the former communist East Germany.

Unter den Linden S-Bahn
S-Bahn Station on Unter den Linden

This S-Bahn station is one of the former "ghost subway" stops. When Berlin was divided during the Cold War, the subway proved to be a challenge. Some lines ran under both West and East Berlin. The East rented these subway lines to the West for 28 years. I remember riding the subway during this time. The train would slow down a little as you approached a subway stop in East Berlin. The stations were lit, mostly maintained, but completely empty (with the exception of the East German soldiers standing guard). Above ground, there was no way to enter the stations as the East German government blocked them off. The stops reopened shortly after the Berlin Wall came down. Notice the old green and white tiles on the walls.

Russische Botschaft
(Russian Embassy)
63-65 Unter den Linden
Not open to the public
S-Bahn: Unter den Linden

You can't miss this huge Stalinist 1950s building, home to the Russian Embassy. It was one of the first large postwar construction projects in East Berlin. Notice the hammer-and-sickle in the cement above the windows. It's built in the style known as "Zuckerbäckerstil" or "wedding-cake style," and you'll understand why when you see it.

Komische Oper Berlin
(Comic Opera Berlin)
41 Unter den Linden
Tel. 202600 (box office)
Admission: Tickets begin at €10
U-Bahn: Französische Strasse/
S-Bahn: Unter den Linden
www.komische-oper-berlin.de

Musical theater, ballet and opera performances (not just comic opera) are held here. The original baroque interior survives, but the exterior is from the 1960s.

SHOPPING TIP

Kunstsalon
41 Unter den Linden
Tel. 20450203
Open daily
U-Bahn: Französische
Strasse/S-Bahn: Unter den
Linden

This strange and interesting shop sells leftovers from Berlin Comic Opera productions and stage memorabilia. You'll find everything from souvenirs to stage props to costumes, although I couldn't find the staff that the fat woman holds at the end of that Wagner opera.

Deutsche Guggenheim Berlin
(German Guggenheim Museum)
13-15 Unter den Linden
Tel. 2020930
Open daily 11am-8pm
(Thur until 10pm)
Admission: €4 (free on Mondays)
U-Bahn: Französische Strasse/
S-Bahn: Unter den Linden
www.deutsche-guggenheim.de

This branch of the famous Guggenheim Museums of contemporary and modern art is located on the ground floor of the Berlin headquarters of Deutsche Bank. You'll find changing exhibits and an emphasis on avant-garde German artists.

Staatsbibliothek
(State Library)
8 Unter den Linden
Tel. 2660
Open Mon-Fri 9am-9pm
(Sat until 5pm)
U-Bahn: Französische Strasse/
S-Bahn: Unter den Linden
www.staatsbibliothek-berlin.de

Catch up on your German reading at this grand library. It houses over 10 million items, including the original sheet music for Beethoven's *Ninth Symphony*.

Humboldt-Universität zu Berlin
(Humboldt University of Berlin)
6 Unter den Linden
Tel. 20930
U-Bahn: Französische Strasse/
S-Bahn: Unter den Linden
www.HU-Berlin.de

Known as the HUB, this is Berlin's first university. Statues of its founders, the brothers Humboldt, are featured prominently on the superb façade. Albert Einstein taught here, and Karl Marx was a student. There's also often an outdoor book market along the sidewalk in front of the school.

Bebelplatz
(Bebel Square)
A square along the Unter den Linden. Across from the Humboldt University of Berlin just before Staatsoper
Open daily
Admission: Free
S-Bahn: Unter den Linden

It was here on May 10, 1933, that the Nazis had their infamous book burning. A monument set into the middle of the square commemorates the event. There's a glass floor where you can see a large underground room with empty shelves symbolizing the 25,000 books by "enemies" of the government that were burned here. Access to the memorial is temporarily closed due to construction in the area.

On the west side of the square is the 18th-century **Alte Bibliothek** (Old Library). Locals nicknamed it "Kommode," which means "chest of drawers." That statue in the center of Unter den Linden is Frederick the Great on his horse.

Deutsche Staatsoper
(German State Opera)
7 Unter den Linden
Tel. 203540.
Tickets: 20354555
Open for events. Ticket sales Mon-Sat 10am-8pm, Sun 2pm-8pm
Admission: Depends on the event
S-Bahn: Unter den Linden/U-Bahn: Französische Strasse or Hausvogteiplatz
www.staatsoper-berlin.org

The original building was destroyed in World War II, and the copy you see today was built in 1955. Locals call it Staatsoper Unter den Linden. This is the home of the German State Opera, an opera company that traces its roots back to the 1700s. If you attend an event, the lavish interior with immense chandeliers and wall paintings will impress. Concerts and ballet are also held here.

Food on the Run Tip:
Opernpalais/Operncafé
5 Unter den Linden
Tel. 202683
Open daily
S-Bahn: Unter den Linden/U-Bahn: Französische Strasse
www.opernpalais.de

Next door to the German State Opera, this café, restaurant and bar located in a former palace has lots of old-world charm. Have some coffee and choose from the selection of delicious cakes and pastries. Around Christmas (usually from December 6 to the 24th), there's a large market here selling traditional German arts and crafts. Moderate.

Deutsches Historisches Museum
(German History Museum)
2 Unter den Linden
Tel. 203040
Open Tues-Sun 10am-6pm
Admission: s2
U-Bahn: Friedrichstrasse
www.dhm.de

This museum is housed in a former armory (the Zeughaus), the oldest building on Unter den Linden. It has a new wing designed by IM Pei who also designed the famous glass-pyramid entrance to Paris's Louvre Museum. Changing exhibits tell the history of Germany.

Neue Wache
(New Guard House)
4 Unter den Linden
Open daily 10am-6pm
Admission: Free
U-Bahn: Friedrichstrasse

This former guard house dates back to 1816 and is now the site of a memorial to the victims of war and tyranny. The remains of both the unknown soldier and unknown concentration camp victims are surrounded by soil from World War II concentration camps and battlefields. Inside is the moving statue by Käthe Kollwitz, *Mother With Her Dead Son.*

Restaurant Tip:
Zur Nolle
203 Georgenstrasse (near Friedrichstrasse)
Tel. 20454280
Open Wed-Mon 11am-6pm
S- and U-Bahn: Friedrichstrasse
www.restaurant-nolle.de

Basic German dishes among the antiques at this popular place. You're in Germany, so have a beer! Inexpensive.

Bahnhof Friedrichstrasse
(Friedrichstrasse Train Station)
Friedrichstrasse at Georgenstrasse
S- and U-Bahn: Friedrichstrasse

This was the main train station for East Berlin. Constructed in 1962, it served as customs for travel between East and West Berlin. It used to be filled with paths and halls that were developed, it seemed, to make the traveler confused while passing through. Its transparent pavilion was deceiving as it truly hid the oppressive parting scenes between those from the West and those from the East who could not cross the border (see the "Palace of Tears" below).

Tränenpalast
(Palace of Tears)
Immediately north of Bahnhof
Friedrichstrasse
17 Reichstagufer
Box office open Wed-Fri 4pm-9pm, Sat and Sun 6:30pm-9pm
S- and U-Bahn: Friedrichstrasse
www.traenenpalast.de

This building, housing a cabaret and beer garden, is where many tears were shed by residents of East Berlin, as this was where they had to say goodbye to their West Berlin relatives and friends who could visit them, but they couldn't cross the wall. It has a huge calendar of events.

Antik & Flohmarkt
(Antique and Flea Market)
Bahnhof Friedrichstrasse (along Georgenstrasse)
Open Wed-Mon 11am-6pm
S- and U-Bahn: Friedrichstrasse

Antiques and lots of junk sold in the arches under the S-Bahn tracks at Friedrichstrasse Station.

Denkmal für die Ermordeten Juden Europas
(Memorial to the Murdered European Jews/Holocaust Memorial)
Ebertstrasse and Behrenstrasse
Phone: 74072929
Open at all times. Information center open daily 10am-8pm
Admission: Free
S-Bahn: Unter den Linden
www.holocaustmahnmal.de

This powerful and massive, five-and-a-half-acres memorial of 2,711 gravestone-like columns honors those Jews killed by the Nazis. It opened in May, 2005, after years of planning and controversy. When you are walking along the cobblestone walkways between the pillars, it is intended to invoke a feeling of being lost, alone and disoriented. The paths between the pillars slope down as you move deeper into the memorial. There's an underground center that includes the known names of those killed in the Holocaust along with letters from those on their way to concentration camps. It's truly a remarkable memorial that recalls the unimaginable.

St. Hedwigs-Kathedrale
(St. Hedwig Cathedral)
3 Hinter der Katholischen

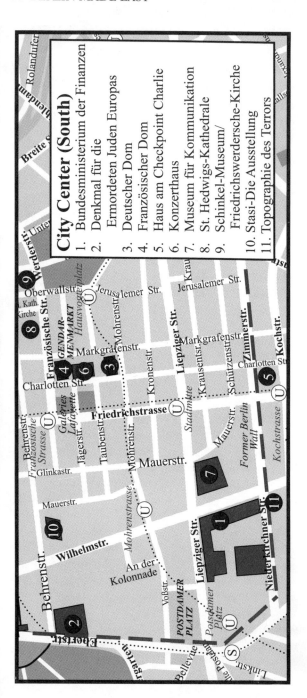

City Center (South)

1. Bundesministerium der Finanzen
2. Denkmal für die Ermordeten Juden Europas
3. Deutscher Dom
4. Französischer Dom
5. Haus am Checkpoint Charlie
6. Konzerthaus
7. Museum für Kommunikation
8. St. Hedwigs-Kathedrale
9. Schinkel-Museum/ Friedrichswerdersche-Kirche
10. Stasi-Die Ausstellung
11. Topographie des Terrors

Kirche
Tel. 2034810
Open Mon-Sat 10am-5pm,
Sun 1pm-5pm
Admission: Free
U-Bahn: Französische Strasse/
Hausvogteiplatz
www.hedwigs-kathedrale.de

This Roman Catholic cathedral was bombed during the war (its modern interior is the result of renovation by the GDR). The circular building dates back to the mid-1700s. The crypt contains the remains of Father Bernhard Lichtenberg, one of the few vocal opponents of the Nazis. He died while being sent off to the concentration camp at Dachau.

Schinkel-Museum/
Friedrichswerdersche-Kirche
(Schinkel Museum/Friedrichswerder
Church)
Werderscher Markt/48 Französische
Strasse
Tel. 2081323
Open Tues-Sun 9am-5pm
Admission: €2
U-Bahn: Hausvogteiplatz
www.smpk-berlin.de

Schinkel, Berlin's most influential architect, designed this church with its twin square towers in the 1820s. Many of his buildings did not survive the war. This former church

SHOPPING TIPS

The Friedrichstadtpassagen is between Französische Strasse and Mohrenstrasse. It's a shopping complex that includes the two stores below, linked by an underground passageway:

Galeries Lafayette
23 Französische Strasse
Tel. 209480
Open Mon-Sat 10am-8pm
U-Bahn: Französische
Strasse
www.galerieslafayette.de

You'll feel like you're in Paris at this Berlin branch of the famous French department store. Don't miss the basement food market filled with French wines, breads, cheese and other French delicacies!

Quartier 206
71 Französische Strasse
Tel. 20946800
Open Mon-Fri 11am-8pm
(Sat 10am-6pm)
U-Bahn: Französische
Strasse
www.quartier206.com

Next door to Galeries Lafayette, this small department store has a beautiful Art Deco interior filled with designer fashions and interesting household goods.

was rehabilitated in the 1980s, and now houses a museum dedicated to the architect and his works.

Restaurant Tips:
Borchardt
47 Französische Strasse
Tel. 81886262
Open daily 11:30am-2am
U-Bahn: Französische Strasse

A French bistro in Berlin. Good food and friendly service are the reasons to visit this very popular, very attractive restaurant located near Gendarmenmarkt. Dining prices vary widely. Moderate – Expensive.

VAU
54-55 Jägerstrasse
Tel. 2029730
Open Mon-Sat noon –2:30pm and 7:30pm-10:30pm
U-Bahn: Französische Strasse

This elegant, long and narrow wood-paneled restaurant is one of Berlin's finest. The international food on its changing menu is excellent and the prices are steep. Very Expensive.

Gendarmenmarkt
(Gendarmen Market)
U-Bahn: Französische Strasse

This beautiful square features

three stunning buildings. The statue in the middle is of Friedrich Schiller, who wrote *William Tell* in 1804.

Konzerthaus
(Concert House)
2 Gendarmenmarkt
Tel. 203090
Open for events
Admission: Depends on the event
U-Bahn: Französische Strasse
www.konzerthaus.de

Flanked by the **Deutscher Dom** and the **Französischer Dom**, the magnificent Konzerthaus has three concert halls in which about 550 events are held annually. This is home to the famous Berlin Symphony Orchestra and the German Symphony Orchestra. The building has been restored to its original 1821 glory.

Französischer Dom
(French Cathedral)
Gendarmenmarkt
Tel. 229-1760
Museum: Open Tues-Sat noon-5pm, Sun 11am-5pm
Tower: Open daily 10am-6pm
Admission: €2
U-Bahn: Französische Strasse
www.franzoesische-kirche.de

The French Cathedral is home to the **Hugenottenmuseum**, which tells the story of the

Huguenots, Protestants who arrived in Berlin after being expelled from France in the late 1600s. The church was heavily bombed in the war, but has been restored. You can climb the spiral staircase to the top of the tower for good views of the city (€3).

Deutscher Dom
(German Cathedral)
1 Gendarmenmarkt
Tel. 22730431
Open Tues-Sun 10am-6pm
Admission: Free
U-Bahn: Französische Strasse
or Stadtmitte
www.deutscherdom.de

This Lutheran cathedral was built in 1708 and is topped by a 23-foot-tall statue of Virtue. It's now the home of exhibits with the theme "Questions on German History."

Food on the Run Tip:
Fassbender & Rausch
60 Charlottenstrasse (at the corner of Mohrenstrasse)
Tel. 20458440
Open Mon-Fri 10am-8pm, Sat 10am-6pm, Sun noon-8pm
U-Bahn: Französische Strasse
www.fassbender-rausch.de

This chocolate shop— Europe's largest! —near the German Cathedral is just the place to stuff your face with great German chocolate. Oh, go ahead!

Museum für Kommunikation
(Museum for Communication)
16 Leipziger Strasse
Tel. 20294204
Open Tues-Fri 9am-5pm, Sat and Sun 11am-7pm
Admission: €3
U-Bahn: Mohrenstrasse
www.museumsstiftung.de/berlin

This is the world's first postage museum. It's pride and joy is one of the rarest stamps in the world, the "Blue Mauritius." Only 500 stamps from this British colony were printed in 1847, and only 12 stamps are known to have survived (6 used and 6 unused). Exhibits feature the history of communication, including the world's first telephone.

Stasi-Die Ausstellung
(Stasi-The Exhibit)
38 Mauerstrasse
Tel. 23247951 or 22417470
Open Mon-Sat 10am-6pm
Admission: Free
U-Bahn: Mohrenstrasse
www.bstu.de

The GDR's Ministry for State Security (Stasi) is featured at this exhibit. It tells the story of the secret police and how their informants attempted to control the lives of all citizens through snitches and wiretaps, among other things. The most bizarre method was the collection of sealed swabs of sweat taken from the groins of interrogated suspects. The Stasi kept over six million files. Celebrities including figure skater Katarina Witt have filed lawsuits to keep the contents of the files secret.

Galerie Max Hetzler
90-91 Zimmerstrasse
Tel. 2292437
Open for exhibits
Admission: Free
U-Bahn: Kochstrasse
www.maxhetzler.com

One of two contemporary art galleries owned by art dealer Max Hetzler featuring interesting exhibits. The other gallery is at 15-18 Holzmarktstrasse in the brick arches of the Jannowitzbrücke S-Bahn station.

Haus am Checkpoint Charlie
(The House at Checkpoint Charlie)
43-45 Friedrichstrasse
Tel. 2537250
Open daily 9am-10pm
Admission: €9.50
U-Bahn: Kochstrasse
www.mauermuseum.de

This was the only checkpoint through which foreigners could pass between East and West Berlin. You really shouldn't leave Berlin without a visit to this spot. The history of the building of the Berlin Wall is documented, along with incredible stories of attempts to escape East Berlin. The checkpoint gets its name from checkpoint number three (as in the military code of Alpha for one, Bravo for two and Charlie for three). Some of the ways that people were smuggled into West Berlin are on display and are very interesting. Attempts to escape included tunnels, hot-air balloons, a mini-submarine, suitcases, and cars with false compartments. There's also a display dedicated to the Berlin Wall's demise in the 1989 peaceful revolution. Come early to avoid crowds, especially on Mondays, when this is one of the few museums open.

Topographie des Terrors
(Topography of Terror)
8 Niederkirchnerstrasse
Tel. 25486703
Open Oct-Apr 10am-dark,
May-Sep 10am-8pm
Admission: Free
U-Bahn: Kochstrasse/
Potsdamer Platz
www.topographie.de

The Prinz Albrecht Palais (the former headquarters of Hitler's Gestapo) once stood here. An exhibit on the history of Nazi terror is appropriately located in what were the cells in the basement of the Gestapo headquarters. This site will soon house four different exhibits related to the infamous history of Nazism.

Bundesministerium der Finanzen
(German Finance Ministry)
Corner of Wilhelmstrasse and Niederkirchnerstrasse at 5-7 Leipziger Strasse/
97 Wilhelmstrasse
Not open to the public
U-Bahn: Kochstrasse/ Potsdamer Platz
www.bundesfinanzministerium.de

This Nazi-era building and former home to the Nazi Air Force (Luftwaffe) survived World War II bombing. It's now the German Finance Ministry. While part of communist East Germany, it housed the Ministry of Ministries (no kidding)! On the north side of the building (on the corner of Wilhelmstrasse and Leipziger Strasse) is an excellent example of communist-era art. A 1950s tiled wall mural features happy laborers singing the praises of communism. Offsetting this image (in the courtyard in front of the mural) is a large faux reflecting pool containing a photograph of a 1953 uprising against communism.

Museumsinsel (Museum Island)

Museumsinsel
(Museum Island)
An island in the Spree River at the eastern end of Unter den Linden
S- and U-Bahn: Friedrichstrasse

Several museums (described below) are all found on this island in the Spree River. It was the original settlement of Berlin, founded in the 13th century. It's been declared a World Heritage site by UNESCO and is undergoing a huge renovation. There's an arts, crafts, clothes and *kitsch* (junk art) market here on

Saturdays and Sundays 9am-3pm.

Bodemuseum
(Bode Museum)
Museumsinsel
Closed for renovation
U- and S-Bahn: Friedrichstrasse/
S-Bahn: Hackescher Markt

This museum will ultimately house the Museum of Byzantine Art, Collection of Antique Sculpture, and Coin Cabinet. It's currently closed for renovation.

Altes Museum
(Old Museum)
Lustgarten (Museumsinsel)
Tel. 20950555
Tues-Sun 10am-6pm
Admission: €8
U- and S-Bahn: Friedrichstrasse/
S-Bahn: Hackescher Markt
www.smb.spk-berlin.de

This museum on the Lustgarten (the "Pleasure Garden"), with its grand neo-Classical façade and fantastic entrance hall, contains a collection of Roman and Greek antiquities, including a portrait of Cleopatra. The museum is now also the home of the **Ägyptisches Museum** (Egyptian Museum) dedicated to the art of ancient Egypt from the royal art collections, with the emphasis on the age

of Queen Nefertiti. The collections include the great "Temple Gate of Kalabasha" (dating back to 20 B.C.), and a piece of papyrus containing the only existing handwriting of Cleopatra. The famous bust of Nefertiti (created over 3,000 years ago and discovered by German archeologists in 1912) will be a highlight of your visit. The Egyptian Museum will move to the Neues Museum (also on Museum Island) before 2010.

Pergamonmuseum
(Pergamon Museum)
Museumsinsel
Tel. 20905577
Open Tues-Sun 10am-6pm (Thur until 10pm)
Admission: €8
U- and S-Bahn: Friedrichstrasse/
S-Bahn: Hackescher Markt
www.smb.spk-berlin.de

Perhaps the best museum in Berlin. The building, which houses one of the world's largest museums of archeology, was completed in 1930. It also houses the **Museum für Islamische Kunst** (Museum of Islamic Art), and has a massive collection of antiquities from the Near East (one of the largest collections of Persian, Babylonian and Assyrian antiquities). Highlights include the Pergamon Altar, a huge (and I do mean huge) altar dating back to 160 B.C. There are 27 steps leading up to this 40-foot-tall colonnaded Greek temple. It was discovered in 1864 in Turkey, and brought to Germany in 1902. You'll also find the superb blue "Gate of Ishtar" dating back to the time of King Nebuchadnezzar in 562 B.C., and the "Market Gate of Miletus" dating back to A.D. 120.

Berliner Dom
(Berlin Cathedral)
1 Am Lustgarten (Museumsinsel)
Tel. 202690
Open Mon-Sat 9am-7pm, Sun noon-7pm
Admission: €5
U- and S-Bahn: Friedrichstrasse/
S-Bahn: Hackescher Markt
www.berlinerdom.de

Berlin's huge Protestant cathedral dates back to the early 1900s, but a church has been here since the 1500s. It was heavily bombed in World War II and remained mostly in ruins until renovation began in the 1970s. Today, the interior of this Italian Renaissance-style cathedral has been restored to its former, and ornate, glory. The views from the stupendous green copper dome are great. Hope you like to climb steps, as there are 270 of them. crypt contains the remains of the House of Hohenzollern, the Prussian rulers from 1701-1918. Frequent concerts are held here featuring the cathedral's 7,000-pipe organ.

Alte Nationalgalerie
(Old National Gallery)
1-3 Bodestrasse (Museumsinsel)
Tel. 20905566
Open Tues-Sun 10am-6pm (Thur until 10pm)
Admission: €8
U- and S-Bahn: Friedrichstrasse/
S-Bahn: Hackescher Markt
www.smb.spk-berlin.de/ang/s.html

Germany's largest collection of 18th-, 19th- and early 20th-century art and sculpture is housed in this impressive building. You'll find works by such notables as Rodin, Manet, van Gogh, Degas, Pissaro, Rodin, Monet, Cézanne and Berlin's own von Menzel.

Neues Museum
(New Museum)
Between the Pergamon Museum and the Altes Museum on Museumsinsel
S-Bahn: Hackescher Markt

This museum will house the Egyptian Museum and the Primeval and Early History 's completed

Palast der Republik
(Palace of the Republic)
Schlossplatz (Museuminsel)
U- and S-Bahn: Friedrichstrasse/
S-Bahn: Hackescher Markt
www.pdr.kultur-netz.de

Can you say 1970s? This unattractive monstrosity, abandoned since the 1990s, is the former home of the parliament of the GDR. There are endless debates about what to do with it. It's now scheduled for demolition and who knows if it will be standing by the time you get here.

Berliner Mauer
(Berlin Wall)
The location of the former Berlin Wall is outlined on the maps in this book
www.wall-berlin.org

After World War II, the Allies divided Berlin into four sectors. The American, French and British sectors became West Berlin, and East Berlin was controlled by the Soviet Union. Between 1949 and 1961, three million people left East Germany. To stop this mass exodus, a 100-mile fence was erected virtually overnight on August 13, 1961, a barrier that remained for 28 years. Ultimately, the concrete wall was 13 feet tall and had a buffer zone (no man's land) of between 25 and 160 feet. Three hundred guard towers were built to monitor the area around the wall. In that 28-year period, 5,043 people are known to have successfully gotten around the wall. Guards fired at 1,693 people and made 3,221 arrests. In all, 1,067 are said to have died trying to flee East Germany, and as many as 263 of the deaths were at the Berlin Wall. Did you know that the GDR referred to the wall as "The Anti-Fascist Protective Rampart"? Guards suspected of shooting to miss were court-marshaled. A total of 52 military officials and 141 border guards were charged with manslaughter or attempted manslaughter for killings at the border, although most were given suspended sentences. Only 11 spent time in prison.

Almost the entire wall is gone, having been chipped away as souvenirs or demolished. A 230-feet-long portion of the wall was reconstructed and includes bits and pieces of the original wall. The "new wall" is mostly stainless steel and contains narrow holes allowing you to look to the other side. It's located at Bernauer Strasse and Ackerstrasse, not too far from the Bernauer Strasse U-Bahn.

A large stretch still stands along Wilhelmstrasse. Behind it is a park on the site of Hitler's SS command center. (See the entry for the Topography of Terror exhibit on pages 22-23).

Alexanderplatz

Alexanderplatz
(Alexander Square)
Between Karl-Liebknecht-Strasse and Grunerstrasse
U- and S-Bahn: Alexanderplatz

The East German government developed this huge square in the 1960s and 1970s

and you can tell! I visited here in the 1980s and it was a weird experience, as the square was then and continues to be both ugly and fascinating. Hideous communist-era buildings are dominated by a huge television tower (see below). The fountain here

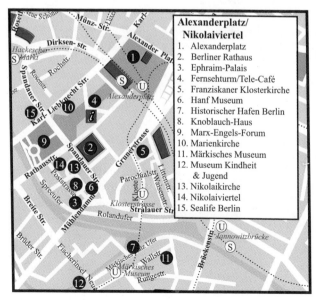

Alexanderplatz/ Nikolaiviertel

1. Alexanderplatz
2. Berliner Rathaus
3. Ephraim-Palais
4. Fernsehturm/Tele-Café
5. Franziskaner Klosterkirche
6. Hanf Museum
7. Historischer Hafen Berlin
8. Knoblauch-Haus
9. Marx-Engels-Forum
10. Marienkirche
11. Märkisches Museum
12. Museum Kindheit & Jugend
13. Nikolaikirche
14. Nikolaiviertel
15. Sealife Berlin

(the one with all the graffiti on it) has a wonderfully communist name: **Brunnen der Völkerfreundschaft** or "Fountain of the Friendship of Peoples." The silly-looking world clock (**Weltzeituhr**) with an atom design on top (you have to see it to understand) will tell you the time in such important communist strongholds as Havana and Hanoi. This plaza, like so many others in Berlin, will soon turn into a large construction zone, as there are plans for skyscrapers to be built here before 2010.

SHOPPING TIP

Kaufhof am Alexanderplatz
9 Alexanderplatz
Tel. 247430
Open Mon-Fri 9am-8pm,
Sat 9am-4pm
U- and S-Bahn:
Alexanderplatz
www.galleriakaufhof.de

The incredibly ugly 1970s façade of this department store is being gussied up. This is East Berlin's oldest and best-known department store. Five floors with stuff similar to what you would find in the KaDeWe department store in West Berlin, but at more reasonable prices.

Fernsehturm
(Television Tower)
Alexanderplatz
(1A Panoramastrasse)
Tel. 2423333
Open Nov-Feb 10am-midnight,
Mar-Oct 9am-1am
Admission: €7
U- and S-Bahn: Alexanderplatz
www.berlinerfernsehturm.de

It only takes a minute to reach the observation deck at the top of this 1,207-foot-tall television tower overlooking Alexanderplatz. Construction was completed in 1969. It's slightly taller than the Eiffel Tower in Paris. Much has been made of the fact that (to the dismay of former communist East German rulers), when at certain times the sun reflects on the tower, the reflection is in the shape of a cross. West Berliners dubbed this phenomenon "The Pope's Revenge." Great views of all of Berlin. If you're lost in Berlin, just look for this spire and it will help you figure out where you are. There's a **Tourist-Information Center** at the base of the tower. Open daily 10am to 6pm with extended hours April through October.

Food on the Run Tip:
Tele-Café
In the Television Tower (Fernsehturm)

Tel. 2423333
Open Nov-Feb 10am-midnight,
Mar-Oct 9am-1am
U- and S-Bahn: Alexanderplatz

Have a snack at this revolving café/restaurant located in the television tower on Alexanderplatz. The restaurant revolves 360 degrees every half hour. Enjoy the view! Moderate.

Marienkirche
(St. Mary's Church)
8 Karl-Liebknecht-Strasse
Tel. 2424467
Open Apr-Oct 10am-6pm, Nov-Mar 10am-4pm
Admission: Free
U- and S-Bahn: Alexanderplatz
www.marienkirche-berlin.de

Parts of this Gothic church date back to 1270. Of note are the baroque pulpit made of marble, the 18th-century organ, and the bronze baptismal font. Right inside the door is a painting dating back to 1475 named *The Dance of Death*. It was discovered under a layer of white paint in 1860. Now, what sort of *Dummkopf* would have thought, "Why, this painting seems very old; I think I'll just paint over it"?

Sealife Berlin
3 Spandauer Strasse

Tel. 992800
Open daily 10am-6pm (Apr-Aug until 7pm)
Admission: €14
U- and S-Bahn: Alexanderplatz
www.sealife.de

This new aquarium is great for kids. There's a popular starfish petting bed and a fantastic glass elevator that you ride through the tanks as you exit. All exhibits are in both German and English.

Berliner Rathaus
(Berlin City Hall)
15 Rathausstrasse
Tel. 90260
Open Mon-Fri 9am-6pm
Admission: Free
U- and S-Bahn: Alexanderplatz

Built in the 1860s, this is still Berlin's town hall (it was East Berlin's town hall during the years of division). It's beautiful both inside and out, although you can see only parts of the inside of the building for security reasons. The frieze features scenes of Berlin's history. It's called **Rotes Rathaus** (Red Town Hall) after the color of its brick, not its former Communist occupants. The fountain outside (**Neptunbrunnen**, which means "Neptune Fountain") dates back to 1891.

Tel. 2415625
Open daily at 11:30am
Reservations recommended
U- and S-Bahn: Alexanderplatz

Large portions of German food are served in old-fashioned dining rooms. There's often live 1920s and 1930s music. *Goulash, Sauerbraten,* and pork are featured on the menu, along with wine and lots of beer. Moderate.

Nikolaiviertel (Nicholas Quarter)

Nikolaiviertel
(Nicholas Quarter)
South of Alexanderplatz
U-Bahn: Klosterstrasse

Named after the St. Nicholas Church (see below), this is Berlin's oldest quarter. The GDR painstakingly reconstructed the remains of the area's medieval and baroque buildings in 1987 in preparation of the 750th anniversary of the city. Stroll the cobblestone streets past the cafés and shops. Among the highlights are the **Ephraim-Palais** (16 Poststrasse) and **Knoblauch-Haus** (23 Poststrasse).

Nikolaikirche
(St. Nicholas Church)
Off of Poststrasse
at Nikolaikirchplatz
Tel. 24724529
Open Tues-Sun 10am-6pm
Admission: Free

U-Bahn: Klosterstrasse
www.stadtmuseum.de

This twin-spired church is Berlin's oldest, dating back to the 13th century. It now hosts changing exhibits.

Restaurant Tip:
Zur Letzten Instanz
14-16 Waisenstrasse
(at Parochialstrasse)
Tel. 2425528
Open Mon-Sat noon-1am, Sun noon-11pm
U-Bahn: Klosterstrasse
www.zurletzteninstanz.de

Dating from 1621, this is Berlin's oldest restaurant. Both Beethoven and Napoleon are said to have eaten here. This restaurant has small wood-paneled rooms occupying two floors of three baroque buildings. Simple German food is served and there's a small beer garden. Moderate.

Hanf Museum
(Hemp Museum)
5 Mühlendamm
Tel. 2424827
Open Tues-Fri 10am-8pm, Sat and Sun noon-8pm
Admission: €3
U-Bahn: Klosterstrasse
www.hanflobby.de/hanfmuseum

Said to be the world's largest museum devoted to the history of hemp (and coincidentally the movement to legalize it, especially the use of medical marijuana). You'll see socks, pretzels, soap, jeans, running shoes and even kitty litter all featuring this versatile herb.

Marx-Engels-Forum
(Mark Engels Forum)
Bounded by the Spree River, Rathausstrasse, Spandauer Strasse and Karl-Liebknecht-Strasse
U-Bahn: Alexanderplatz

Erich Honecker, the former head of the GDR, dedicated this large square in the mid-1980s to Karl Marx and Friedrich Engels, the (as he called them) "greatest sons of the German people." Bigger-than-life-size statues of them are here, along with stainless-steel blocks featuring the struggles of the world's workers.

Franziskaner Klosterkirche
(Franciscan Cloister Church)
73-74 Klosterstrasse
Tel. 636-1213
Open at all times
Admission: Free
U-Bahn: Klosterstrasse
www.klosterruine-berlin.de

Formerly a Franciscan monastery, this Gothic church is being restored from ruins.

Historischer Hafen Berlin
(Historical Harbor Berlin)
Märkisches Ufer (southern tip of Museumsinsel)
Tel. 21473257
Open Tues-Fri 2pm-6pm, Sat and Sun 11am-6pm
Admission: €2
U-Bahn: Märkisches Museum
www.historischer-hafen-berlin.de

The Historical Harbor is an outdoor boat museum on the southern tip of Museum Island.

Märkisches Museum
(Markisch Museum)
5 Am Köllnischen Park
Tel. 30866215
Open Tues-Sun 10am-6pm (Wed until 8pm)

Admission: €4
U-Bahn: Märkisches Museum
www.stadtmuseum.de

This museum follows the history of Berlin from the Bronze Age to today.

Museum Kindheit & Jugend
(Museum of Childhood and Youth)
32 Wallstrasse
Tel. 275-0383

Open Tues-Fri 9am-5pm, Sat and Sun 10am-6pm
Admission: €2 (adult), €1 (child)
U-Bahn: Märkisches Museum
www.berlin-kindheitundjugend.de

This museum is dedicated to the history of childhood life in Berlin, and is known for its large collection of historical toys and its exhibit recreating a 100-year-old Berlin classroom.

Scheunenviertel

Scheunenviertel
North of the Spree River with Friedrichstrasse to the east and Hackescher-Markt to the west

This area historically was Berlin's Jewish quarter. It has changed the most of any neighborhood since reunification and is a vibrant and exciting area for tourists. It, along with neighboring Prenzlauer Berg, is my favorite area of the city.

Dokumentationszentrum Berliner Mauer
(Berlin Wall Memorial Site)
111 Bernauer Strasse
Tel. 4641030

Tues- Sun April-Oct 10am-6pm, Nov-Mar 10am-5pm
Admission: Free
U-Bahn: Bernauer Strasse
www.berliner-mauer-dokumentationszentrum.de

This site is located north of Mitte (Center) along Bernauer Strasse. Although mostly in German, this memorial, document center and museum tells the story of a neighborhood divided by a man-made structure. A portion of the wall still stands here. Poignant scenes were played out here as, overnight, residents found their neighbors across the street on the other side of the wall.

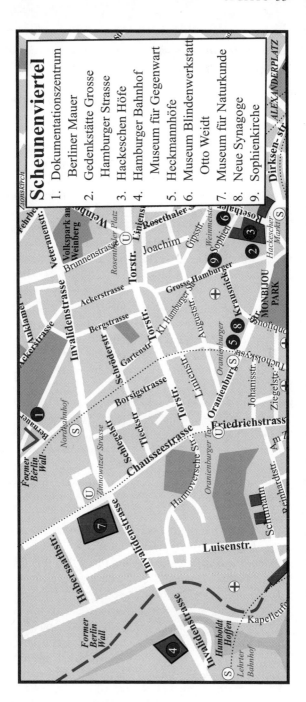

Scheunenviertel

1. Dokumentationszentrum Berliner Mauer
2. Gedenkstätte Grosse Hamburger Strasse
3. Hackeschen Höfe
4. Hamburger Bahnhof Museum für Gegenwart
5. Heckmannhöfe
6. Museum Blindenwerkstatt Otto Weidt
7. Museum für Naturkunde
8. Neue Synagoge
9. Sophienkirche

Museum für Naturkunde
(Natural History Museum)
43 Invalidenstrasse
Tel. 20938591
Open Tues-Fri 9:30am-5pm,
Sat and Sun 10am-6pm
Admission: €4
U-Bahn: Zinnowitzer Strasse
www.museum.hu-berlin.de

This large natural-history museum has bragging rights to the largest dinosaur skeleton in the world. Lots of taxidermied animals, rocks and fossils.

Hamburger Bahnhof Museum für Gegenwart
(Hamburg Station Museum of Contemporary Art)
50-51 Invalidenstrasse
Tel. 39783411
Open Tues-Fri 10am-6pm, Sat 11am-8pm, Sun 11am-6pm
Admission: €6
S-Bahn: Lehrter Bahnhof
www.hamburgerbahnhof.de

One of Germany's best collections of modern art is showcased in the Hamburger Bahnhof, a former train station. You'll likely recognize Andy Warhol's famous 1975 portrait of Chinese Chairman Mao.

Neue Synagoge
(New Synagogue)
28-30 Oranienburger Strasse
Tel. 88028451
Open Sept-Apr Sun-Thur 10am-6pm, Fri 10am-2pm, May-Aug Mon and Sun 10am-8pm, Tues-Thur 10am-6pm, Fri 10am-5pm
Admission: €3
S-Bahn: Oranienburger Strasse
www.cjudaicum.de

The new synagogue is not new at all. It once held 3,200 people, and was topped by a huge Moorish dome. It dates back to the 1850s, and has had a history of repeated destruction beginning with the infamous "Night of Broken Glass," also known as "Crystal Night" (*Kristallnacht*) on November 9, 1938, when Jewish businesses, synagogues and homes were attacked by Nazi mobs. Fire destroyed many buildings, and many Berlin Jews lost their lives in the upheaval. This was an early chapter in the Nazi plan to exterminate the Jews of Europe.

It was further damaged by Allied bombs and demolished in the 1950s by the East German government. It's been partially restored, including its turquoise and gold dome. Ground markers outline the original structure. An exhibit tells the sad history of Berlin's Jewish community.

Heckmannhöfe
(Heckmann Courtyards)
32 Oranienburger Strasse
Open daily
S-Bahn: Oranienburger Strasse

This courtyard complex has shops and restaurants in a converted machine factory.

Restaurant Tip:
QBA
45 Oranienburger Strasse
Tel. 28040505
Open daily
S-Bahn: Oranienburger Strasse

Am I in Havana? Cuba was a huge trading partner with the former East Germany, so many East Berliners are familiar with Cuban food. This hectic, loud bar and restaurant serves Cuban specialties and drinks. Inexpensive – Moderate.

Hackeschen Höfe
(Hackian Courtyards)
At Oranienburger Strasse and Rosenthaler Strasse
Open daily
Admission: Free
S-Bahn: Hackescher-Markt
www.hackesche-hoefe.com

This building complex with eight linked courtyards (which survived the bombings and East German neglect) was built in 1907. The beautiful ceramic façades have been restored, and the complex is now home to cafés, theaters, restaurants, boutiques and galleries. A fine example of Art Nouveau industrial architecture. Check out the **Ampelmänn Shop** in courtyard number four for souvenirs.

Restaurant Tip:
Hackescher Hof
40/41 Rosenthaler Strasse
Tel. 2835293
Open daily Mon-Sun noon-4pm and 6pm-2am
S-Bahn: Hackescher-Markt
www.hackescher-hof.de

This restaurant has an outdoor café in the Hackeschen Höfe courtyard. A wonderful place to have soup, a salad and a drink. Great people watching, too. Moderate.

HISTORY UNDER FOOT

In the area around the Hackeschen Höfe, you'll find small square bronze plaques set into the sidewalks. These contain the name, date of deportation, and concentration camp where each person died.

Gedenkstätte
Grosse Hamburger Strasse
(Grosse Hamburger Strasse
Jewish Memorial)
26 Grosse Hamburger Strasse
Open daily
Admission: Free
S-Bahn: Hackescher-Markt

Stark and haunting, this memorial features statues of gaunt deportees on the site where Jews were held prior to deportation to concentration camps. Tradition has it that you place a stone on the memorial marker as a sign of remembrance. At numbers 15-16 on this street you'll find an empty lot once occupied by a house destroyed during World War II bombing. It's now the site of "The Missing House,"

with plaques containing the names and professions of its former residents.

Sophienkirche
(Sophien Church)
29 Grosse Hamburger Strasse
Tel. 3087920
Open daily (hours vary)
Admission: Free
U-Bahn: Weinmeisterstrasse
www.sophien.de

This baroque church in a charming neighborhood, completed in 1713, is named after Queen Sophie Luisa, the third wife of King Friedrich I.

Restaurant Tip:
Sophieneck
37 Grosse Hamburger Strasse
Tel. 2822109
Open Mon-Sun noon-2am
Admission: Free
U-Bahn: Weinmeisterstrasse
www.sophieneck-berlin.de

Comfortable   corner restaurant serving regional and international dishes. Moderate.

Museum Blindenwerkstatt Otto Weidt
(Museum Blind Workshop Otto Weidt)
39 Rosenthaler Strasse
Tel. 28599407
Open Mon-Fri noon-8pm, Sat and Sun 11am-8pm

SHOPPING TIP

Schönhauser Design
18 Neue Schönhauser
Strasse
Tel. 2811704
Open Mon-Fri noon-8pm,
Sat 11am-5pm
www.schoenhauser-
design.de

Yearning for the "good old days" of life in communist East Germany? This store stocks everything from furniture to groovy lamps to 1980s sunglasses.

Admission: €2
www.blindes-vertrauen.de

This small museum tells the story of Otto Weidt who, during Nazi rule, courageously protected the deaf and blind Jewish employees of his brush and broom business.

Restaurant Tip:
Rocco
In the arches beneath Hackescher-Markt S-Bahn
Tel. 246386063
Open daily
S-Bahn: Hackescher-Markt

A restaurant/bar under the railroad viaducts at the Hackescher Markt station. The interior is stunning, with carved wood and a brick vaulted ceiling. Basic Italian and German fare, including pizzas. Great people watching at the café. Inexpensive – Moderate.

SHOPPING TIP

Rosenthaler Platz
(Rosenthal Square)
Off of Rosenthaler Strasse
S-Bahn: Rosenthaler Strasse

Many diverse stores, especially clothes shops, are found on the small streets around this square.

Prenzlauer Berg

Prenzlauer Berg
Northeast of the central city
(Mitte)

This neighborhood in former East Berlin is fast becoming a trendy area with many fine restaurants.

Wasserturm
(Water Tower)
Corner of Knaackstrasse and

Rykestrasse
Closed to the public
U-Bahn: Senefelderplatz

This circular water tower is one of Prenzlauer Berg's main landmarks. Constructed in 1875, the Nazis used its basement as a torture chamber. It now houses apartments. Locals call it "Dicker Hermann" which means, "fat Hermann."

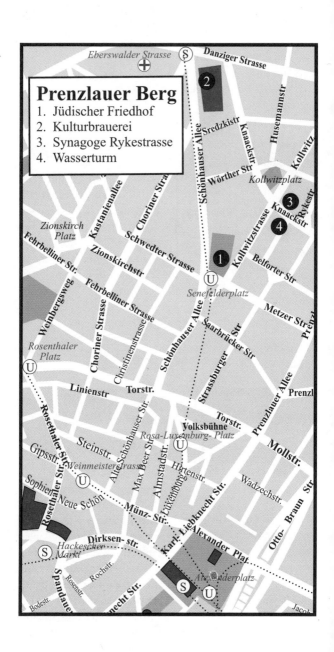

Eberswalder Strasse ⊕ Ⓢ Danziger Strasse

2

Prenzlauer Berg
1. Jüdischer Friedhof
2. Kulturbrauerei
3. Synagoge Rykestrasse
4. Wasserturm

Sredzkistr

Schönhauser Allee

Knaackstr

Husemannstr

Kollwitz

Wörther Str

Kollwitzplatz

Choriner Stra

3

Knaackstr

Rykestr

4

Zionskirch Platz

Kastanienallee

Schwedter Strasse

Kollwitzstrasse

Belforter Str

Fehrbelliner Str

Zionskirchstr

1

Ⓤ

Metzer Stra

Prenz

Weinbergsweg

Choriner Strasse

Fehrbelliner Strasse

Christinenstrasse

Schönhauser Allee

Saarbrücker Str

Senefelderplatz

Rosenthaler Platz

Ⓤ

Strassburger Str

Prenzlauer Allee

Linienstr

Torstr.

Choriner Strasse

Torstr.

Prenzl

Rosenthaler Str.

Steinstr.

Alte Schönhauser Str.

Rosa-Luxemburg- Platz

Volksbühne

Ⓤ

Mollstr.

Gipsstr.

Weinmeisterstrass

Ⓤ

Max Beer Str

Almstadtstr.

Hirtenstr.

Wadzechstr.

Otto- Braun Str

Sophienstr

Neue Schön

Münz- Str.

Luxemburg

Karl- Liebknecht Str

Dirksen- str.

Hackescher Markt

Ⓢ

Rochstr.

Alexander Plat.

Rosenstr.

Spandaue

knecht Str.

Ⓢ Ⓤ

Alexanderplatz

Bodestr.

Jacob

Synagoge Rykestrasse
(Rykestrasse Synagogue)
53 Rykestrasse
Open only for services
U-Bahn: Senefelderplatz

This is the only Berlin synagogue that survived *Kristallnacht* and World War II bombing. It's the largest in Germany, and served as the sole synagogue in former East Berlin. Its interior, however, was vandalized, and it was even used as a stable for horses at one time.

Jüdischer Friedhof
(Jewish Cemetery)
23-25 Schönhauser Allee
Tel. 4419824
Open Mon-Thur 10am-4pm,
Fri 10am-1pm
Admission: Free
U-Bahn: Senefelderplatz

As you wander this shaded and somewhat gloomy Jewish cemetery (which survived Nazi vandalism), you can contemplate, "why?"

Kulturbrauerei
(Cultural Brewery)
36-39 Schönhauser Allee
Open daily
Admission: Free
www.kulturbrauerei-berlin.de

The yellow- and red-brick buildings of a former brewery

JEWISH

Denkmal für die Ermordeten Juden Europas
(Memorial to the Murdered European Jews)
Ebertstrasse and Behrenstrasse
Neue Synagoge
(New Synagogue)
28-30 Oranienburger Strasse
Jüdisches Museum Berlin
(Jewish Museum Berlin)
9-14 Lindenstrasse
Jüdischer Friedhof
(Jewish Cemetery)
23-25 Schönhauser Allee
Haus der Wannsee-Konferenz
(House of the Wannsee Conference)
56-58 Am Grossen in Wannsee
Sachsenhausen Concentration Camp
22 Strasse der Nationen in Oranienburg

dating back to the mid-1800s are now home to taverns, cinemas, clubs and a supermarket. You can take a look at East German product design (especially from the 1950s) at the special-interest museum **Sammlung Industrielle Gestaltung** (Collection of Industrial Design) near the

...ain entrance of the complex.

Restaurant Tips:
Trattoria Paparazzi
35 Husemannstrasse
Tel. 4407333
No credit cards
Open daily 6pm-1am
U-Bahn: Eberwalder Strasse

Popular *trattoria* serving hearty Italian fare at reasonable prices. Friendly service. Moderate.

Gugelhof
37 Knaackstrasse
Tel. 4429229
Open Mon-Fri 4pm-1am, Sat and Sun 10am-1am
U-Bahn: Eberwalder Strasse/

Senefelderplatz
www.gugelhof.de

Comfortable and friendly restaurant serving Alsatian food. A favorite of locals and tourists (including Bill Clinton). Moderate.

Zeiss-Grossplanetarium
(Zeiss Planetarium)
80 Prenzlauer Allee
Tel. 42184512
Open Mon-Fri 9am-noon, Wed and Sat 1:30pm-9pm, Fri 7pm-9pm, Sun 1:30pm-5pm
Admission: €5
S-Bahn: Prenzlauer Allee
www.astw.de

This large planetarium has changing exhibits.

Friedrichshain

Friedrichshain
The neighborhood southeast of the central city (Mitte)
U-Bahn: Warschauer Strasse

Large sections of this neighborhood did not escape the concrete-block housing favored by the communist government. The **East Side Gal**lery along the Spree River near Warschauer Strasse is home to the longest remaining stretch of the Berlin Wall. The beautiful bridge over the Spree River is the **Oberbaumbrücke**. It was closed for many years as it sat on the edge of the Berlin Wall. Just south of the bridge is

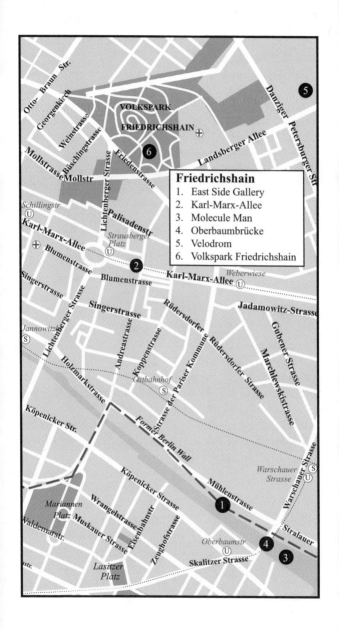

Friedrichshain

1. East Side Gallery
2. Karl-Marx-Allee
3. Molecule Man
4. Oberbaumbrücke
5. Velodrom
6. Volkspark Friedrichshain

Molecule Man, a huge aluminum sculpture by American artist Jonathan Borofsky.

Karl-Marx-Allee
(Karl Marx Avenue)
The street coming off of the southeast of Alexanderplatz
S- and U-Bahn: Alexanderplatz (other U-Bahn stops along the street are Schillingstrasse, Strausberger Platz and Weberwiese)

This long and extremely wide street was formerly called "Stalinallee" until it was renamed by the GDR (when Stalin fell out of favor). Before World War II, it was called "Frankfurter Allee." The Soviet Army entered Berlin along this street at the end of World War II and nearly everything surrounding it was destroyed. The grand buildings that line the avenue today are excellent examples of Communist-era architecture and building styles. Historical markers in both German and English line the street. There's an information center at Café Sybille at number 72. You'll feel like you're in Eastern Europe.

Volkspark Friedrichshain
(Friedrichshain Public Park)
Am Friedrichshain and Friedenstrasse
U-Bahn: Strausberger Platz

This is Berlin's oldest park and home to the **Märchenbrunnen** ("Fairytale Fountain"), featuring figures from the Brothers Grimm fairytales. There are also two memorials here. One is dedicated to Polish and German resistance to the Nazis, and the other to German soldiers who fought in the Spanish Civil War against fascism. Those big mounds are some of the "rubble mountains" found in Berlin, created from all the rubble left behind after World War II.

ENTERTAINMENT TIPS

Friedrichshain is home to a huge nightlife scene. Venues and bars change frequently. If you're into late-night action, DJs and cover charges, try the following, but remember they are all far outside the city center:

Astro
40 Simon-Dach-Strasse, Tel. 7682625
Lee Harvey Oswald Bar
68 Grünberger Strasse, Tel. 44017400
Panorama Bar
70 Rüdersdorfer Strasse, Tel. 29000597

Velodrom
(Velodrome: Cycling Center)
26 Paul-Heyse-Strasse
Tel. 44304430 (tickets)
Open for events
S-Bahn: Landsberger Allee
www.velodrom.de

Although designed for cycling, this modern circular venue also hosts other sporting events and concerts.

Potsdamer Platz

Potsdamer Platz
(Potsdam Square)
Southeast of the Tiergarten
U- and S -Bahn: Potsdamer Platz
www.potsdamer-platz.net

Bombed beyond recognition in World War II, this square found itself in former East Berlin. It was unused and undeveloped while the city was divided. After reunification, it was transformed into the commercial heart of the city and is filled with innovative architecture, including the DaimlerCity complex.

Sony Center
At Potsdamer Platz on Potsdamer Strasse
U- and S -Bahn: Potsdamer Platz
www.sonycenter.de

This steel-and-glass entertainment complex is home to tons of movie theaters and cafés. It has a fantastic glass-and-textile ceiling in its central forum, which is interestingly lit in the evening. The elegant **Kaisersaal Café** of the former Grand Hotel Esplanade has been moved here.

Filmmuseum Berlin
(Film Museum Berlin)

SHOPPING TIP

Potsdamer Platz Arkaden
(Potsdam Square Arcade)
At the Potsdamer Platz U-Bahn and S-Bahn stations
U- and S -Bahn: Potsdamer Platz
www.potsdamer-platz.net/ arkaden

Over 100 stores on three levels at this shopping mall.

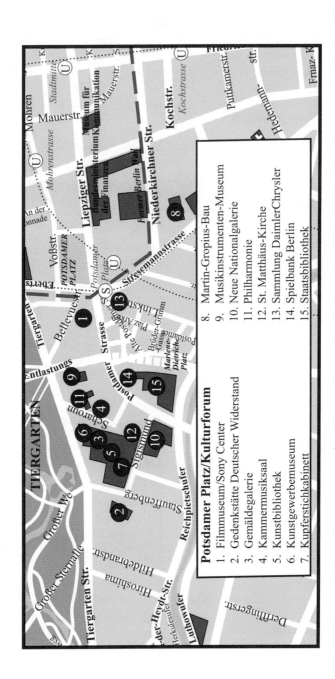

Potsdamer Platz/Kulturforum

1. Filmmuseum/Sony Center
2. Gedenkstätte Deutscher Widerstand
3. Gemäldegalerie
4. Kammermusiksaal
5. Kunstbibliothek
6. Kunstgewerbemuseum
7. Kupferstichkabinett
8. Martin-Gropius-Bau
9. Musikinstrumenten-Museum
10. Neue Nationalgalerie
11. Philharmonie
12. St. Matthäus-Kirche
13. Sammlung DaimlerChrysler
14. Spielbank Berlin
15. Staatsbibliothek

2 Potsdamer Strasse at Potsdamer Platz (Sony Center)
Tel. 3009030
Open Tues-Sun 10am-6pm (until 8pm on Thur)
Admission: €6.
U- and S -Bahn: Potsdamer Platz
www.filmmuseum-berlin.de

Located on two floors of the Sony Center, this museum is devoted to the history of German film. Even if you're not a film buff, you'll find much of interest here. There's a room devoted to Marlene Dietrich, German's best-known film star. There's a two-story-tall video screen showing scenes from adventure films. One exhibit features Leni Riefenstahl, the controversial film director known best for her Nazi propaganda film *Triumph of the Will*. The film library now has nearly 10,000 films. Berlin is host to an international film festival every February (www.berlinale.de).

Sammlung DaimlerChrysler
(DaimlerChrysler Collection)
5 Alte Potsdamer Strasse
Tel. 25941420
Open daily 11am-6pm
Admission: Free
U- and S -Bahn: Potsdamer

Platz
www.sammlung.daimlerchrysler.com

It's amazing that the 1912 building **Weinhaus Huth** (Huth Wine House) survived World War II and the Berlin Wall. It houses a gallery on the fourth floor of some of the 1,300 pieces of contemporary art owned by the DaimlerChrylser company. In front of the building is a bicycle statue, one of the many sculptures and artwork placed in this area by DaimlerChrylser, including those by Haring, Koons and di Suvero.

Restaurant Tip:
Diekmann
5 Alte Potsdamer Strasse
Tel. 25297524
Open daily
www.j-diekmann.de

This restaurant is housed in the beautiful Weinhaus Huth (Huth Wine House), the only building on Potsdamer Square to survive the war and demolition of the postwar era. Good international fare and attentive service. Interesting wine list. Moderate.

Spielbank Berlin
(Berlin Casino)
1 Marlene Dietrich Platz (Potsdamer Platz)
Tel. 255990

Open daily 11:30am-3am
Admission: €2
U- and S -Bahn: Potsdamer Platz
www.spielbank-berlin.de

Bring your passport and lots of money so you can gamble at Berlin's flashy casino.

Restaurant Tip:
Dietrich's
1 Marlene Dietrich Platz (in the Hyatt Hotel)
Tel. 25531234
U- and S -Bahn: Potsdamer Platz

This modern and popular bar and bistro is named after Hollywood star and Berlin native Marlene Dietrich. It serves some great burgers. Moderate.

Kulturforum
(Cultural Forum)
Just west of Potsdamer Platz
U- and S -Bahn: Potsdamer Platz
www.smpk.de

Since reunification, combining Germany's extensive collection of art (and where to house that art) has been an incredible process. Collections of some of the world's best art are found in the museums located here. Before reunification, the Kulturforum was designed to be West Berlin's rival to East Berlin's Museumsinsel.

Gemäldegalerie
(Picture Gallery)
40 Stauffenbergstrasse at Matthäikirchplatz
Tel. 2662101
Open Tues-Sun 10am- 6pm (Thur until 10pm)
Admission: €6. Free English audio guide
U- and S -Bahn: Potsdamer Platz
www.smb.spk-berlin.de

This incredible museum is located at the Kulturforum, just west of Potsdamer Platz. There are 72 rooms filled with one of the world's greatest collections of European art from the 13th to the 18th century.

Works by greats of the art world such as Botticelli, Corregio, Titian, Raphael, van Eyck, Rubens, Vermeer and Hals are all here. The octagon-shaped Rembrandt room has sixteen of his best works. One section is devoted to Italian painting from the 13th to the 16th century. Other sections are devoted to Dutch and Flemish painting of the 15th, 16th and 17th centuries. Another section exhibits German paintings from late Gothic and Renaissance times. There's a huge selection of Italian, French, German and English paintings of the 18th century. Truly one of the greatest art museums in the world.

Kunstbibliothek
(Art Library)
6 Matthäikirchplatz
Tel. 2662029
Open Tues- Fri 10am-6pm, Sat and Sun 11am-6pm
Admission: €6. Free English audio guide
S- and U-Bahn: Potsdamer Platz
www.smb.spk-berlin.de

An extensive collection of commercial art, posters and engravings are housed in this library.

Kupferstichkabinett
(Drawing and Print Collection)
6 Matthäikirchplatz
Tel. 2662002
Tues to Fri 10am-6pm, Sat and Sun 11am-6pm
Admission: €6. Free English audio guide
U- and S -Bahn: Potsdamer Platz
www.kupferstichkabinett.de

A collection of engravings, drawings, woodcuts and prints, including those by Rembrandt, Picasso and Schinkel.

Philharmonie
(Philharmonic Hall)
1 Herbert-von-Karajan-Strasse
Tel. 25488999 (box office)
Box office open daily 9am-6pm
Admission: Tickets begin at €20
U- and S -Bahn: Potsdamer Platz
www.berliner-philharmoniker.de

The Philharmonie is the home of the Berlin Philharmonic Orchestra, one of the world's best. A modern venue for a superb symphony. No seat in this concert hall is more than 100 feet from the stage. Next door is the **Kammermusiksaal** (Chamber Music Hall).

Musikinstrumenten-Museum
(Musical Instrument Museum)
1 Tiergartenstrasse
at Matthäikirchplatz
Tel. 254810
Open Tues-Fri 9am-5pm (Thur until 10pm), Sat and Sun 10am-5pm
Admission: €3
U- and S -Bahn: Potsdamer Platz
www.mim-berlin.de

A large collection of musical instruments is housed in this museum (the white building to the east of the Philharmonie). The grand Wurlitzer organ is a highlight. The collection comes to life during 11a.m. Saturday tours.

Kunstgewerbemuseum
(Museum of Arts and Crafts)
6   Tiergartenstrasse   at Matthäikirchplatz
Tel. 2662902
Open Tues-Fri 10am-6pm, Sat and Sun 11am-6pm
Admission: €6
U- and S -Bahn: Potsdamer Platz
www.smb.spk-berlin.de

This huge museum is located across from the Philharmonie, and has a collection of decorative arts and crafts from the Middle Ages (especially silver and gold medieval religious objects) through the 20th century. There are large collections of Art Nouveau, Art Deco, and Venetian hand blown glass and figurines that you'd hate to have to dust! Descriptions only in German.

Neue Nationalgalerie
(New National Gallery)
50 Potsdamer Strasse
Tel. 2662662
Open Tues-Fri 10am-6pm, Sat and Sun 11am-6pm
Admission: €6
U- and S -Bahn: Potsdamer Platz
www.smb.spk-berlin.de

An outstanding collection of modern art featuring German (such as Ernst) and international (such as Munch and Dalí) artists is showcased in this modern glass-and-steel building. Frequent special exhibits. Check out the quiet sculpture garden.

Staatsbibliothek
(State Library)
33 Potsdamer Strasse
Tel. 2660
Open Mon-Fri 9am-9pm, Sat 9am-7pm
Admission: Free
U- and S -Bahn: Potsdamer Platz
www.staatsbibliothek-berlin.de

The state library of Germany is one of the largest in Europe and has a substantial selection of books in English.

St. Matthäus-Kirche
(St. Matthew's Church)
Matthäikirchplatz
Tel. 2621202
Open Tues-Sun noon-6pm
Admission: Free. Tower: €1
U- and S -Bahn: Potsdamer Platz

This neo-Romanesque church with a red-brick and ochre-tile façade looks a little out of place in the middle of all the modern buildings in the Kulturforum. It dates back to the mid-1800s, and you can climb the tower for good views of the Kulturforum and the Tiergarten. Frequent concerts are held here.

Gedenkstätte Deutscher Widerstand
(German Resistance Memorial)
13-14 Stauffenbergstrasse
Tel. 2699-5000
Mon-Fri 9am-6pm (Thur until 8pm), Sat and Sun 10am-6pm
Admission: Free. English audio guide €3
U- and S -Bahn: Potsdamer Platz
www.gdw-berlin.de

This museum and memorial (south of the Tiergarten and to the west of Kulturforum) is dedicated to the Germans who resisted Hitler. There are plays and films about the Resistance every Sunday at 11 a.m.

Martin-Gropius-Bau
(Martin Gropius Building)
7 Niederkirchnerstrasse
Tel. 254860
Open hours vary
Admission: Depends on exhibit
U- and S -Bahn: Potsdamer Platz

This magnificent building is home to changing exhibits on art, architecture and photography. It's named after the architect who designed the building in the 1880s.

Tiergarten

Tiergarten
Open daily
Admission: Free
S-Bahn: Tiergarten

This 412-acre park is so huge that sometimes it's hard to believe that you're in the middle of a large metropolis. It was opened to the public in

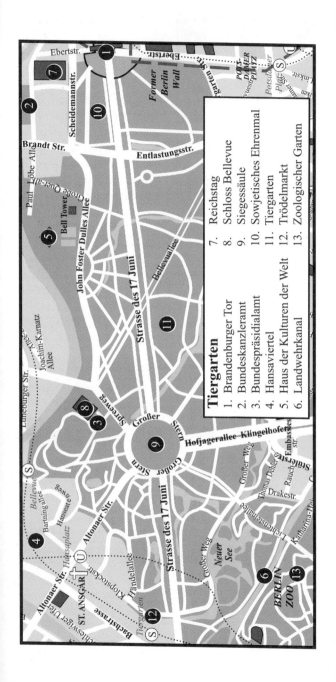

Tiergarten

1. Brandenburger Tor
2. Bundeskanzleramt
3. Bundespräsidialamt
4. Hansaviertel
5. Haus der Kulturen der Welt
6. Landwehrkanal
7. Reichstag
8. Schloss Bellevue
9. Siegessäule
10. Sowjetisches Ehrenmal
11. Tiergarten
12. Trödelmarkt
13. Zoologischer Garten

the 1700s and is filled with walkers, runners and, in good weather, Berliners having picnics and sunbathing. There's a lovely canal here, the **Landwehrkanal**. Most of its trees were lost in the winter of 1945-1946 after World War II to those desperate for firewood, but you'd never know it today.

At the east end of Strasse des 17. Juni (the park's main street) is the **Sowjetisches Ehrenmal** (Soviet War Memorial). The two tanks here are said to be the first tanks to enter Berlin at the end of the war. When Berlin was split, this memorial was in the "British Zone," but was still guarded by Soviet soldiers. All the roads and paths in the park lead to another memorial, the **Siegessäule** (Victory Column) (in the center of Strasse des 17. Juni) commemorating Prussian military victories against France, Austria and Denmark. The Goddess of Victory tops this red-granite column. You can climb the spiral staircase to reach an observation platform with good views of the park and the surrounding area (€3).

At the north end of the park is a small palace, the **Schloss**

Bellevue. This is the home of the German president. The modern, oval-shaped building just south of here is the **Bundespräsidialamt**, where Germany's president has his office. The park is a great place to get away from the bustling city. The name means "Animal Garden," as this was originally the royal hunting preserve.

Food on the Run Tip:
Schleusenkrug
At the west end of the Tiergarten near the train station Bahnhof Zoologischer Garten on Müller-Breslau-Strasse
Tel. 3139909
Open daily 10am-1am
U- and S -Bahn: Zoologischer Garten
www.schleusenkrug.de

Take a break at this informal restaurant/beer garden along the canal in the park and have a great German beer.

Trödelmarkt
(Flea Market)
Near the corner of Strasse des 17. Juni and Bachstrasse (west end of Tiergarten)
Open Sat and Sun 10am-5pm
Admission: Free
S-Bahn: Tiergarten

If you get off at the S-Bahn Tiergarten on the weekends,

you'll be at this interesting flea market. Tons of junk, but you can find some interesting souvenirs, too. Also, lots of food stands.

Restaurant Tip:
First Floor
45 Budapester Strasse (in the Palace Berlin Hotel)
Tel. 25021020
Mon-Fri and Sun noon-3pm and 6pm-10:30pm, Sun 6pm-10:30pm
U-Bahn: Zoologischer Garten
www.palace.de

Located on the floor above street level at the Palace Berlin Hotel near the Tiergarten, this restaurant earns rave reviews for both food (German and French cuisine) and service. Expensive.

Zoologischer Garten Berlin
(Berlin Zoo)
8 Hardenbergplatz
Tel. 254010
Zoo open daily from March 15-Oct 14 9am-6:30 pm and Oct 15-Mar14 9am-5pm
Aquarium open daily 9am-6pm
Admission: €10
U- and S- Bahn: Zoologischer Garten
www.zoo-berlin.de

The southwest part of the Tiergarten is home to Germany's oldest and largest

zoo. You'll find 15,000 animals, an aquarium, petting zoo, a huge birdhouse–and giant pandas, the zoo's biggest attraction. Its aquarium has three floors of every imaginable fish, reptile, insect and amphibian. It's known for its crocodile exhibit.

Haus der Kulturen der Welt
(House of World Cultures)
10 John-Foster-Dulles-Allee
Tel. 397870
Open Tues-Sun 9am-9pm
Admission: Depends on the exhibit
S-Bahn: Unter den Linden
www.hkw.de

Exhibits dedicated to world culture, from art to film, are held here. The building (formerly the Congress Hall or Kongresshalle) was a gift from the United States and opened in 1958. Locals call it the "pregnant oyster" because of its odd shape.

Reichstag
(Parliament Building)
Platz der Republik
Tel. 22732152
Open daily (entry through metal detectors) from 8am-midnight (you must enter before 10pm)
Admission: Free
S-Bahn: Unter den Linden
www.bundestag.de

The seat of the German Parliament tells the story of Germany and Berlin. This neo-Renaissance building was constructed between 1884 and 1894. The inscription on the front of the building says "Dem Deutschen Volke" ("To the German People"). Fire broke out here in 1933 and destroyed much of it. It's believed that followers of Hitler started it, but the Communists were blamed. This infamous event allowed Hitler to round up and arrest "enemies" of the government. Allied bombing heavily damaged it at the end of World War II. You can still see graffiti carved by Soviet soldiers on the interior walls. Most of the ornamentation and the central dome were removed after the war during reconstruction, and the building was not used from 1933 to 1999. It sat forlornly near the Berlin Wall. In 1995, the artist Christo wrapped the entire building in fabric. It remained "wrapped" by scaffolding for four years while being rebuilt. The building took on new meaning after reunification when Berlin was restored as the capital of Germany, and, since April 1999, the Reichstag is again the seat of the Bundestag (the German parliament).

Today's design is by British architect Sir Norman Foster, who added a fantastic glass dome. Light enters the dome and reflects off 360 mirrors in the dome. The dome can be reached by taking the elevator. You then walk up spiral ramps to the top (there's also a rooftop restaurant). At night, the dome is lit from inside. The lobby features a huge 60-foot German flag. Modern buildings housing federal government offices flank the Reichstag.

Bundeskanzleramt
(Federal Chancellery)
1 Willy-Brandt-Strasse
Closed to the public
S-Bahn: Lehrter Bahnhof

This huge complex of modern buildings to the north of the Reichstag and at the northern tip of the Tiergarten (along the Spree River) is home to the Federal Chancellery.

Hansaviertel
(Hansa Quarter)
U-Bahn: Hansaplatz

Those interested in architecture should come to this neighborhood to the north of Tiergarten. This area was completely demolished in World War II. In the late

1950s, the International Builder's Exhibition coordinated the design of this area. Fifty architects from 22 countries designed these innovative buildings. But if you're not interested in architecture, you'll be bored.

Schöneberg/Kreuzberg

Schöneberg/Kreuzberg
South of the Tiergarten and Mitte

Trendy Schöneberg is home for many of Berlin's gay residents, and Kreuzberg's residents are an interesting mix of young professionals and a large number of Turks.

Deutsches Technikmuseum Berlin
(German Museum of Technology)
9 Trebbiner Strasse
Tel. 902540
Open Tues-Fri 9am-5:30pm, Sat and Sun 10am-6pm
Admission: €5
U-Bahn: Möckernbrücke
www.dtmb.de

Great for kids, the large German Museum of Technology is jammed with everything from old computers to U-boats. Lots of interactive exhibits that make science in-teresting. You can't miss the building. It's the one with the American airplane hanging from it. Special sections are devoted to shipping, railroads and aircraft.

Jüdisches Museum Berlin
(Jewish Museum Berlin)
9-14 Lindenstrasse
Tel. 25993300
Open Mon 10am to 10pm and Tues to Sun 10am to 8pm
Admission: €5
U-Bahn: Kochstrasse
www.jmberlin.de

The building housing this museum is itself worth the trip. Representing a shattered Star of David, the theme here is disorientation, emptiness and darkness. This museum tells the story of Germany's Jews–from contributions to German society to inclusion into German life to the devastating forced exclusion. The architect has left "voids" (hol-

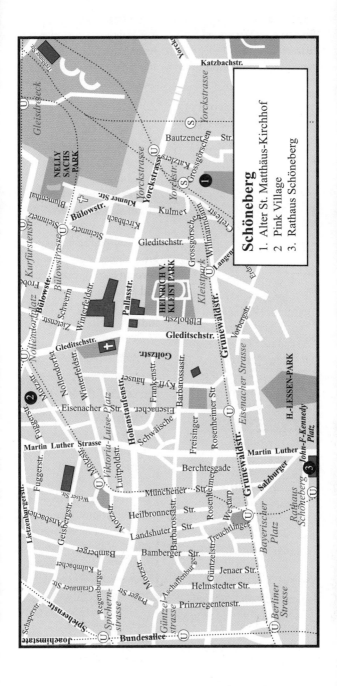

Schöneberg

1. Alter St. Matthäus-Kirchhof
2. Pink Village
3. Rathaus Schöneberg

low portions of the museum) to represent the huge loss of life and the loss to the German people as a result of the Holocaust.

SHOPPING TIP

Ararat
99A Bergmannstrasse
Tel. 6935080
Open Mon-Fri 10am-8pm,
Sat 10am-4pm
U-Bahn: Gneisenaustrasse

This is just the kind of place where you can spend way too much time. It has a huge selection of postcards, everything from vintage travel postcards of Berlin to 1980s postcards featuring Linda Ronstadt. There's also a good selection of souvenirs, stationery and gifts.

Chamissoplatz
(Chamisso Square)
Between Arndtstrasse and Willibald-Alexis-Strasse
Open daily
Admission: Free
U-Bahn: Platz der Luftbrücke

To experience Berlin as it looked before it was bombed, visit this beautifully restored square. There's an organic food market here every Saturday morning.

Restaurant Tip:
For a wide variety of ethnic restaurants, visit the lively **Bergmannstrasse**. *U-Bahn: Bergmannstrasse.*

Viktoriapark
(Victoria Park)
South of Yorckstrasse between Katzbachstrasse and Mehringdamm
U-Bahn: Platz der Luftbrücke or Yorckstrasse

This leafy park, complete with artificial waterfall, is a great place to take a break. Its paths wind to the summit where there is a memorial to victories in the Napoleonic Wars, and great views of all of Kreuzberg.

SHOPPING TIP

Diverse and interesting shops selling everything from antiques to designer clothing are found on Eisenacher Strasse. *U-Bahn: Nollendorfplatz.* Produce, flowers, prepared foods, and crafts can all be found at Winterfeldtplatz, *Wed. and Sat. 8am-1pm. U-Bahn: Nollendorfplatz.*

Schwules Museum
(Homosexual Museum)
61 Mehringdamn

Tel. 69599050
Open Wed-Mon 2pm-6pm
(Sat until 7pm)
Admission: €5
U-Bahn: Mehringdamm
www.schwulesmuseum.de

Homosexuals were rounded up by the Nazis during World War II, forced to wear pink triangles, and sent to concentration camps. Amsterdam's Homomonument was the first monument dedicated to the struggle of homosexuals for equal rights. This museum, opened in 1985, is the first museum in the world dedicated to gay life. Temporary exhibits are housed on the ground floor. This is also a research center housing thousands of books, periodicals, films, and photographs in its archives and library.

Pink Village/Gay and Lesbian Berlin

U-Bahn: Nollendorfplatz
w w w . b e r l i n - t o u r i s t -
i n f o r m a t i o n . d e / e n g l i s h /
zielgruppen

Berlin has long had an active gay community, and has even elected a gay mayor. The area around the Nollendorfplatz (especially Motzstrasse) is the center of gay life. A granite pink-triangle plaque at the Nollendorfplatz U-Bahn re-

members the gay victims of Nazi rule. There's a gay information center for men, Man-o-Meter at 5 Motzstrasse, and for women, Lesbenberatung eV at 20A Kulmer Strasse. There's a huge gay-pride celebration the last weekend of June called Christopher Street Day, and a large street fair and celebration in late June (Lesbisch-Schwules Stadfest). There are also many gay establishments in Prenzlauer Berg, especially in the area around the U-Bahn Schönhauser Allee. Here are a few café/bars in the area:

•**Hafen**, *19 Motzstrasse, Tel. 21141180 (men)*
•**Tom's**, *19 Motzstrasse, Tel 2134570 (men)*
•**Begine**, *139 Potsdamer Strasse, Tel. 2151414 (women)*

Restaurant Tips:
More
28 Motzstrasse
Tel. 23635702
Open 9am-midnight
U-Bahn: Nollendorfplatz
www.more-berlin.de

You don't have to be gay to enjoy the innovative dishes at this gay-owned restaurant. Friendly service. Moderate.

Carib
30 Motzstrasse
Tel. 2135381

Open 5pm-1am
U-Bahn: Nollendorfplatz
www.carib-berlin.de

Tired of all that German food? Why not try some jerk chicken, coconut beef and exotic cocktails at this Caribbean restaurant. Moderate.

Alter St. Matthäus-Kirchhof
(Old St. Matthew's Churchyard)
12 Grossgörschenstrasse
Open 8am-8pm in the summer, 8am-4pm in the winter
Admission: Free
U- or S-Bahn: Yorckstrasse

Among the famous buried in this cemetery are the Brothers Grimm, and the conspirators in the failed attempt to kill Hitler in 1944.

Rathaus Schöneberg
(Schöneberg Town Hall)
John-F-Kennedy-Platz
Tel. 78760
Open daily 9am to 6pm. Tower open daily 10am to 5pm (tower closed Nov. to March.)
Admission: Free
U-Bahn: Rathaus Schöneberg (near second-to-the-last stop on U-Bahn line number 4)

It was here in 1963 (at the height of the Cold War) that John F. Kennedy made one of the most memorable speeches of any U.S. President. This speech included: "All free men, wherever they may live, are citizens of Berlin and, therefore, as a free man, I take pride in the words 'Ich

BERLIN AIRLIFT

At the end of World War II, under the terms of the Yalta Agreement, Berlin was divided into four zones controlled by the United States, France, Great Britain and the Soviet Union. In 1948, the Soviet Union, concerned that Berlin would elect an anti-communist city government, cut ties with the committee that administered the city. In June of 1948, all transportation to West Berlin was cut off by the Soviets. The only link between West Germany and West Berlin (which was totally surrounded by Soviet-controlled East Germany) were three air corridors. Allied planes were forced to supply food, supplies and fuel. This became known as "The Berlin Airlift." This blockade lasted eleven months, when the Soviets, having failed to starve the West Berliners, gave up.

bin ein Berliner.'" It doesn't matter that (as countless grammarians have pointed out) he should have said "Ich bin Berliner." His use of "ein Berliner" means "I am a doughnut." Too bad some remember this speech because of its mistake rather than for its humanitarian message, including "Freedom is indivisible, and when one man is enslaved, all are not free." You can climb the tower for great views. The bell that's rung here every day at noon was a gift from the U.S. in the 1950s, and is a replica of the Liberty Bell. Inside the town hall is an exhibit with signatures of over 17 million U.S. citizens who signed documents to show support for the citizens of West Berlin during the Berlin Airlift. Only come here if you're a history buff.

Restaurant Tips:
Abendmahl
9 Muskauer Strasse
Tel. 612-5170
No credit cards. Open daily 6pm-1am
U-Bahn: Görlitzer Bahnhof
www.abendmahl-berlin.de

Imaginative vegetarian and fish dishes with irreverent titles. The restaurant's name is a reference to *The Last Supper*. That's why there's a religious-kitsch decor. Moderate.

Türkenmarkt
(Turkish Market)
Maybachufer
Open Tues and Fri noon-6pm
U-Bahn: Schönleinstrasse or Kottbusser Tor

Berlin is said to have the fourth-largest Turkish population in the world. You'll find exotic foods at reasonable prices along with household goods and fabrics here at this bustling market. Get ready to bargain!

Restaurant Tip:
Il Casolare
30 Grimmstrasse
Tel. 69506610
Open daily (hours vary)
U-Bahn: Südstern or Kottbusser Tor

Ask locals in Kreuzberg where to eat inexpensively, and they'll likely send you to this Italian restaurant. Basic dishes such as *gnocchi* and pizzas are served outside along the canal, or inside, surrounded by graffiti-covered walls. Be warned: Service can range from adequate to downright neglectful. Inexpensive.

Kurfürstendamm (Ku'damm)

Kurfürstendamm
*U-Bahn: Uhlandstrasse or
Kurfürstendamm*

This street (thankfully referred to as Ku'damm) is the main shopping street of what used to be West Berlin. Intersecting with Ku'damm is Fasanenstrasse, where you'll find the city's most upscale shops. You know, Gucci, Tiffany…

Food on the Run Tip:
Ku'damm 195
*195 Kurfürstendamm
Tel. 8818942
Open Mon-Thur 11am-5pm,
Fri and Sat 11am-6pm, Sun
noon-5pm
U-Bahn: Uhlandstrasse*

Stand-up snack bar where you can mix with locals while you order everything from *currywurst* (sausage with curry powder or in a curry sauce) to champagne. A popular place for a snack. Inexpensive.

The Story of Berlin
*207-208 Kurfürstendamm (at
Uhlandstrasse)
Tel. 88720100 (reservations)*

*Open daily 10 am to 6pm
Admission: €10
U-Bahn: Uhlandstrasse
www.story-of-berlin.de*

You can wander around this huge multimedia exhibit for hours. The history of Berlin is told in 20 rooms, featuring everything from the plague to the collapse of the Berlin Wall. It's really quite well done. I liked the segment on a typical day in the life of a former resident of East Berlin. There's an English audio guide and labels in English. Interestingly, the exhibit sits on the site of a still-functioning nuclear-bomb shelter built underneath the Ku'damm Karree shopping center in the early 1970s to protect 3,562 people (guided tours hourly). The airplane wing outside is from one of the U.S. Air Force bombers that supplied West Berlin during the Berlin Airlift.

Restaurant Tip:
**Wintergarten: Café
im Literaturhaus**
*23 Fasanenstrasse
Tel. 8825414*

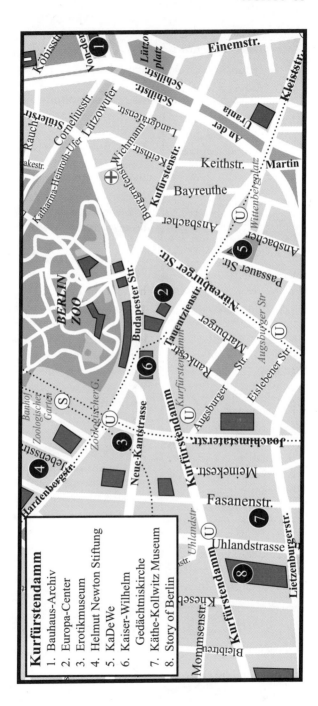

Kurfürstendamm
1. Bauhaus-Archiv
2. Europa-Center
3. Erotikmuseum
4. Helmut Newton Stiftung
5. KaDeWe
6. Kaiser-Wilhelm Gedächtniskirche
7. Käthe-Kollwitz Museum
8. Story of Berlin

SHOPPING TIPS

Leysieffer
218 Kurfürstendamm
Tel. 6001548
Open daily Mon-Sat 10am-7pm, Sun 11am-6pm
U-Bahn: Uhlandstrasse
www.leysieffer.de

Looking for small gifts to take home? This shop sells German chocolates, pastries, coffee and tea. It's located in the former Chinese Embassy.

Wertheim
231 Kurfürstendamm
Tel. 880030
Open Mon-Fri 9:30am-8pm, Sat 9am-8pm
U-Bahn: Kurfürstendamm

This department store on Ku'damm is a great place to pick up what you forgot to pack. It's cheaper than the luxury department store KaDeWe (but owned by them). It has a nice souvenir selection and a restaurant (on the top floor) with good views. There's also a grocery store in the basement complete with champagne bar.

Open daily 9:30am-1am
U-Bahn: Uhlandstrasse

Bring your favorite book and relax in this attractive restaurant overlooking a lovely garden. Moderate.

Käthe-Kollwitz Museum
24 Fasanenstrasse
Tel. 8825210
Open Mon and Wed-Sun 11am to 6pm
Admission: €5 (English pamphlet €5)
U-Bahn: Uhlandstrasse
www.kaethe-kollwitz.de

Who? Kollwitz, who died in 1945, lost both her son and grandson in the World Wars. This museum is located in a villa south of Ku'damm and exhibits the artist's works (including etchings, sculpture and woodcuts). She was a pacifist, and her works here vividly reflect the horrors of war.

Food on the Run Tip:
Loretta Im Garten (Pupasch)
89 Lietzenburger Strasse
No phone
Open daily from 11am to 3 am
Closed Nov. to March
U-Bahn: Uhlandstrasse

A beer garden in the middle of the city. There's a children's play area, and grill stands selling delicious casual food. Inexpensive.

Kaiser-Wilhelm
Gedächtniskirche
*(Kaiser Wilhelm Memorial
Church)*
Breitscheidplatz
Tel. 2185023
Open daily 9am-7pm
Admission: Free
U-Bahn: Kurfürstendamm
www.gedaechtniskirche.com

One of the most recognizable
of all of Berlin's sights. Allied
bombs in the last days of
World War II demolished all
but a few walls and the bell
tower of the Kaiser Wilhelm
church, which had stood here
since the late 1800s. It's a
moving reminder of the destruction this city has seen. In
1961, a new octagonal-shaped
church with blue stained-glass
windows was built beside the
ruins. There's a museum here
telling the story of the old
church, the bombing of the
church and surrounding areas, and the construction of
the new church.

Europa-Center
(Europe Center)
*Down the street from the Kaiser
Wilhelm Memorial Church
along Tauentzienstrasse*
Tel. 26497940
*Admission: Free. €2 to the ob-
servation deck*
*U-Bahn: Kurfürstendamm,
Zoologischer Garten or*
Wittenbergplatz
www.europa-center-berlin.de

You'll find three levels of
shops along with bars,
restaurants, movie theaters
and clubs in this 22-story
building. Great views from
the observation deck. There's
a **Tourist-Information
Center** here *(enter at 45
Budapester Strasse. Open daily
10am to 6pm with extended
hours April through October)*

KaDeWe (Kaufhaus
des Westens)
21-24 Tauentzienstrasse
Tel. 21210
*Open Mon-Fri 10am-8pm, Sat
9:30am–8pm*
U-Bahn: Kurfürstendamm
www.kadewe.de

This huge luxury shopping
center has an incredible buf-
fet-style food hall (the largest
in Europe) on the sixth floor
with over thirty places to eat.
German regional specialties
can be found at all prices. You
can sample over 1,300 types
of cheese, 1,200 sausages and
cold cuts, 240 desserts, 400
types of bread and rolls and
2,400 wines from five continents. Don't miss it!

Erotikmuseum
(Erotic Museum)
4 Joachimstaler Strasse

Tel. 8860666
Open daily 9am-midnight
Admission: €4
U-Bahn: Kurfürstendamm
www.erotikmuseum.de

Eroticism from Greco-Roman times to today is featured at this popular museum. Everything from erotic art to ancient phallic symbols. One exhibit pays tribute to Beate Uhse. She fought for the right to sell sex-related goods in Germany, and has made quite a fortune doing so. Of course, there are the obligatory video stalls for your viewing pleasure and a large store selling sex toys.

Helmut Newton Stiftung/ Museum für Fotografie
(Helmut Newton Foundation/ Museum of Photography)
2 Jebensstrasse (behind the Zoologischer Garten train station)
Tel. 20905566
Open Tues-Sun 10am-6pm (Thur until 10pm)
Admission: €6
S- and U-Bahn: Zoologischer Garten

This former library is now home to over 1,000 photographs of the Museum of Photography and fashion photographer Helmut Newton.

Restaurant Tip:
Marjellchen

9 Mommsenstrasse
Tel. 8832676
Open Mon-Sat 5pm-midnight
Reservations recommended
U-Bahn: Savignyplatz

This quaint restaurant specializes in the cuisine of East Prussia. Not for those looking for light dining! You'll find traditional specialties such as *Mecklenburger Kümmelfleisch* (lamb with onions and chives) on the menu. There's a great wine shop and snack bar next door. Moderate.

Bauhaus-Archiv
(Bauhaus Museum of Design)
14 Klingelhöferstrasse
Tel. 2540020
Open Wed-Mon 10am-5pm
Admission: €6
U-Bahn: Nollendorfplatz
www.bauhaus.de/english

The Bauhaus school of design stressed that form should follow function. The school was founded in 1919 in Germany, but was forced to close in 1933 during the start of the Nazi regime. Its influence on architecture, however, can still be seen worldwide. This museum of architectural design and photography is housed in a Bauhaus school building. A must for those interested in design.

Charlottenburg

Schloss Charlottenburg
(Charlottenburg Palace)
Luisenplatz and Spandauer
Damm
Tel. 32091275
Open Tues–Fri 9am-5pm, Sat
and Sun 10am-5pm
Admission: €12
U-Bahn: Richard-Wagner-
Platz or Sophie-Charlotte-
Platz
www.spsg.de

Can you say "excess"? King Friedrich I had this massive "house" built in the late 1600s as a summer retreat for his wife Sophie Charlotte. Over the years, additions by subsequent kings increased its size. It's sort of Berlin's version of Versailles outside of Paris. Like so many other historic buildings in Berlin, it was severely damaged in World War II, but reconstructed. The highlights include:

The statue of King Friedrich I on his horse as you enter.

The dome topped by a golden statue of Fortune.

The luxurious apartments of King Friedrich and Sophie Charlotte in the **Altes Schloss** (Old Palace), including the over-the-top **Reception Chamber** with mirrored walls and tapestries dating back to the early 1700s, and the incredible collection of porcelain from China in the **Porcelain Chamber**.

The **Neue Flügel** (New Wing), also known as the Knobeldorff-Flügel, contains the apartments of Frederick the Great (Friedrich II) and the **Hohenzollern-Museum**, featuring a selection of items from the royal collection.

The **Neue Pavillon** (New Pavilion), also known as the Schinkel Pavillon after the wing's architect, was constructed in 1825 as an Italianate villa. It houses its own art museum containing mostly early 19th-century works by Berlin artists.

Note that you must take a guided tour to visit certain attractions.

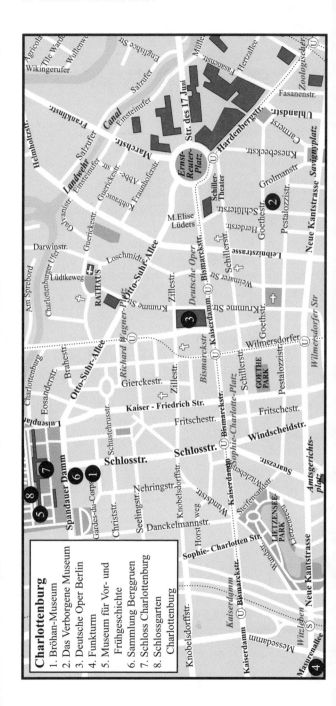

Charlottenburg
1. Bröhan-Museum
2. Das Verborgene Museum
3. Deutsche Oper Berlin
4. Funkturm
5. Museum für Vor- und
   Frühgeschichte
6. Sammlung Berggruen
7. Schloss Charlottenburg
8. Schlossgarten
   Charlottenburg

Restaurant Tip:
Bierhaus Luisen-Bräu
1 Luisenplatz
(near Charlottenburg Palace)
Tel. 3419388
Open daily 9am-midnight
U-Bahn: Richard-Wagner-Platz or Sophie-Charlotte-Platz

Looking for fine dining? Don't come here. But do try this beer hall for it buffet table filled with hearty German dishes, indoor and outdoor dining where you sit at picnic tables with others, and the beer is always flowing. Inexpensive.

Schlossgarten Charlottenburg
(Charlottenburg Palace Gardens)
Luisenplatz
Tel. 32091275
Open daily Mar-Oct 6:30am-8pm, Nov-Feb 6:30am-6pm
Admission: Free
U-Bahn: Richard-Wagner-Platz or Sophie-Charlotte-Platz

Wander these formal, huge French-style gardens established in 1697. You'll see swans swimming in small lakes, the **Mausoleum** containing the remains of many members of the Prussian royal family, and **Belvedere**, the royal teahouse, housing an extensive collection of 18th-century porcelain.

Bröhan-Museum
(Bröhan Museum)
1A Schlossstrasse
Tel. 32690600
Open Tues-Sun 10am-6pm
Admission: €5
U-Bahn: Richard-Wagner-Platz or Sophie-Charlotte-Platz
www.broehan-museum.de

Karl Bröhan was a professor who amassed this huge collection of Art Nouveau and Art Deco objects, paintings and furnishings. (German Art Nouveau is called "Jugendstil.") Exhibits in German only.

Museum für Vor- und Frühgeschichte
(Museum of Primeval and Early History)
Luisenplatz (to the left if you are facing Schloss Charlottenburg)
Tel. 32674811
Open Tues-Fri 9am-5pm, Sat and Sun 10am-5pm
Admission: €6
U-Bahn: Richard-Wagner-Platz or Sophie-Charlotte-Platz
www.smb.spk-berlin.de

This museum follows the evolution of man from 1,000,000 BC to the Bronze Age, from Stone-Age tools to finds from the ancient city of Troy. It's located in a former royal theater built in 1789.

Sammlung Berggruen:
Picasso und seine Zeit
(The Berggruen Collection: Picasso and His Era)
1 Schlossstrasse
Tel. 3269580
Open Tues to Sun 10am to 6pm
Admission: €6
U-Bahn: Richard-Wagner-Platz or Sophie-Charlotte-Platz
www.smpk.de

This museum contains the private collection of Heinz Berggruen, an art dealer. Herr Berggruen had the sense to leave Germany in 1936. He returned 60 years later with this incredible collection. The vast majority of the works here are by Picasso, but you'll also see works by such notables as van Gogh, Matisse, Klee and Cèzanne.

Deutsche Oper Berlin
(German Opera Berlin)
35 Bismarckstrasse/10 Richard-Wagner-Strasse
Tel. 3438401 (box office)
Open for concerts
Admission: Tickets begin at €20
U-Bahn: Deutsche Oper or Bismarckstrasse/S-Bahn: Savignyplatz
www.deutscheoperberlin.de

This opera house in Charlottenburg was built in 1961 and is home to the German Opera. It also is the

venue for dance performances.

Restaurant Tip:
Mar y Sol
5 Savignyplatz
Tel. 3132593
Open daily 11am-1:30am
S-Bahn: Savignyplatz
www.marysol-berlin.de

Great people-watching at this *tapas* bar on a lovely square. Dine indoors, or outdoors on the tiled terrace next to a small fountain. Friendly service. Moderate.

Das Verborgene Museum
(The Hidden Museum)
70 Schlüterstrasse
Tel. 3133656
Open Thur and Fri 3pm-7pm, Sat and Sun for exhibits
Admission: €6
U-Bahn Ernest-Reuter-Platz/ S-Bahn: Savignyplatz
www.dasverborgenemuseum.de

The small "Hidden Museum" (enter through the peaceful courtyard) features the works of early 20th-century German women artists, most of whom were forced into exile or hiding, or were killed by the Nazis who found their works inappropriate.

Funkturm
(Radio Tower)
22 Messedamm

Tel. 30382996
Open daily 10am-11pm (closes at 9pm on Mondays). Restaurant closed Mondays
Admission: €4
U-Bahn: Theodor-Heuss-Platz

What's the Eiffel Tower doing in Berlin? This 454-foot-tall steel structure (surrounded by the International Conference Center) was based upon the Eiffel Tower and com-pleted in 1924. Locals call it "*langer Lulatsch*" which means "lanky lad." You can take the elevator to the observation deck for a panoramic view of Berlin, especially the **Forst Grunewald** (Grunewald Forest). Its Art Nouveau restaurant dates back to 1926. Frankly, don't make a special trip to see this less interesting version of the tower in Paris.

Off the Beaten Path

Dahlemer Museen
(Dahlem Museum Complex)
8 Lansstrasse
Tel. 8301438
Open Tues-Fri 10am-6pm, Sat and Sun 11am-6pm
Admission: €4
U-Bahn: Dahlem-Dorf

This huge complex, located in the Freie Universität, houses several important museums.

Ethnologisches Museum
(Museum of Ethnology)

Exhibits feature what is recognized as the greatest ethnological collection in the world, including important finds from Latin America (Aztec, Incan and Mayan collections), the South Seas, Africa and the Far East.

Museum für Indische Kunst
(Museum of Indian Art)

Features art and artifacts from India, Thailand, Indonesia and Tibet.

Museum für Ostasiatische Kunst
(Museum of Far East Art)

Features Japanese, Chinese and Korean archeological and decorative art.

**Museum
Europäischer Kulturen**
(Museum of European Cultures)

Changing exhibits explore how Europeans, and especially Germans, have lived through the ages.

Brücke-Museum
(The Bridge Museum)
9 Bussardsteig
Tel. 8312029
Open Wed-Mon 11am-5pm
Admission: €4. Special exhibits: €5
U-Bahn: Oskar-Helene-Heim
www.bruecke-museum.de

This small museum is dedicated to the work of "Die Brücke" which means "The Bridge," the name given to the Expressionism movement in Germany, which rejected the modern-art movement of the early 20th century. It's known for its paintings of landscapes, and if you're interested in expressionist art, you should make the trip out to this museum.

Alliierten Museum
(Allied Museum)
135 Clayallee (at Huttenweg)
Tel. 8181990
Open Thur-Tues 10am-6pm
Admission: Free

U-Bahn: Oskar-Helene-Heim
www.alliiertenmuseum.de

In 1945, troops of the United States, France, Great Britain and the Soviet Union marched into Berlin. Soon after, conflict began as the Western countries wanted to rebuild Berlin and Germany as a democracy while the Soviet Union had other ideas. Berlin became the center of the Cold War. This museum is located in what used to be a cinema used by U.S. troops. Exhibits feature the Berlin Airlift and Checkpoint Charlie (the original guard cabin is here), and are in German, English and French (but not Russian!).

Olympiastadion
(Olympic Stadium)
3 Olympischer Platz
Tel. 25002322
Open daily 10am-7pm (summer), 10am-4pm (winter)
Admission: Free. Museum: €3. Tours of stadium on non-event days: €2
U-Bahn: Olympia-Stadion
www.olympiastadion-berlin.de

The Summer Olympic games were held here in 1936. Hitler hoped it would demonstrate Aryan superiority, but was forced to stand by and watch

U.S. runner Jesse Owens win four gold medals. There's now a nearby street named Jesse-Owens-Allee. The stadium is part of a huge park with over 300 acres. Sporting events and concerts are held here. The huge field to the west of the stadium (**Maifeld**) can hold a half-million people, and was frequently used for Nazi mass rallies. It's an excellent example of fascist-era architecture. You can visit the huge stadium, its observation platform, and an exhibit of its history.

Glockenturm
(Bell Tower)
Olympischer Platz
Tel. 3058123
Open daily Apr-Oct 9am-6pm
Admission: €2.50
U-Bahn: Olympia-Stadion
www.glockenturm.de

The observation platform on top of the Bell Tower at Olympic Stadium has great views of not only the stadium, but also to Spandau in the west, all the way to Alexanderplatz to the east and, on a clear day, as far away as Potsdam.

Treptower Park
Along the Spree southeast of the center
Open daily

Admission: Free
S-Bahn: Treptower Park

This quiet and secluded park southeast of the city center is a popular place for runners and hikers. Berlin's second-largest park (the Tiergarten is the largest) was designed in 1874 as an English garden. It's best known for the interesting and thought-provoking memorial to fallen Soviet Union soldiers (**Sowjetisches Ehrenmal**). Thousands of Soviet soldiers died in the battle for Berlin. The memorial stands on the site of a mass grave where 5,000 Soviet soldiers are buried. There's a granite statue of "Mother Russia" grieving for her lost children, and a viewing platform flanked by two triangles of red granite. Overlooking it all is a huge statue of a Soviet soldier holding a child in one hand and destroying a swastika with the other. Another attraction here is the "Molecule Man," an aluminum sculpture that stands in the Spree River. At the edge of the park is Germany's biggest observatory.

Forst Grunewald
(Grunewald Forest)
Southwest of the central city
S-Bahn: Grunewald

A huge (nearly 20 square

miles) and popular forest located southwest of the central city. Runners, walkers, dog walkers and sunbathers (along the small lake **Teufelsee**) all love this green oasis. That hill is **Teufelsberg**, the largest and tallest of Berlin's *Bunkerberge* (rubble mountains), created from all the rubble left behind after World War II bombing.

Haus der
Wannsee-Konferenz
(House of the
Wannsee Conference)
56 Am Grossen Wannsee
Tel. 8050010
Open daily 10am-6pm
Admission: Free
S-Bahn: Wannsee. Bus 114
will take you the rest of the way
www.ghwk.de

Most come to Wannsee to swim and relax at **Strandbad Wannsee**, Europe's largest inland beach (called the "Berlin Riviera"). Wannsee was also the site of one of the most notorious meetings ever held. It was at this mansion on January 20, 1942, that the Head of the Reich Security Office chaired a meeting of fourteen high-ranking Nazi civil servants and SS officers. The purpose of the meeting was to organize and implement "The Final Solution," the decision to deport European Jews and to murder them. The meeting, well-documented in minutes taken by Adolf Eichmann, has become known as "The Wannsee Conference." Today, the house is a memorial to the Holocaust. Grim and gripping official Nazi photographs document life in the concentration camps and medical experiments performed by the Nazis. A haunting memorial. Exhibits in German only.

Botanischer Garten
(Botanical Garden)
6-8 Königin-Luise-Strasse
Tel. 83850100
Museum: Open daily 10am to 6pm
Garden: Open daily 9am to dusk
Admission: €5
S-Bahn: Botanischer Garten (it's a 15-minute walk from the S-Bahn to the garden)
www.bgbm.org

This huge botanical garden (over 100 acres) near the Dahlem Museum Complex has 16 greenhouses, and is filled with nearly 20,000 exotic plants.

Zitadelle Spandauer
(Spandau Citadel)
Am Juliusturm
Tel. 354944200

Open Tues-Fri 9am-5pm, Sat and Sun 10am-5pm
Admission: €4
U-Bahn: Zitadelle
www.zitadelle-spandau.net

The fort is the oldest building in Berlin. A museum

documents (in the many sides of the citadel. It's northwestern Berlin at the juncture of the Spree and Havel rivers.

Excursions

Sachsenhausen Museum
(Sachsenhausen Concentration Camp)
22 Strasse der Nationen in Oranienburg
21 miles (35 km) from Berlin
At the end of the S1 S-Bahn line in the direction of Oranienburg (50-minute trip from Potsdamer Platz). Make sure you buy a ticket that includes zones "ABC." From the train station in Oranienburg, it's approximately a 20-minute walk (look for the signs that say "Gedenkstätte Sachsenhausen"). Bus 804 departs hourly from the square in front of the Oranienburg train station if you don't want to or can't walk to the site.
Tel. 03301/200200
Open daily Mar 15-Oct 14 8:30am-6:00pm, Oct 15-Mar 14 8:30am-4:30pm. The museums at the site are closed on Mondays

Admission: Free (English audio guides available). English pamphlet is €0.50
www.gedenkstaette-sachsenhausen.de

The inscription on the gate reads (as on other concentration camps) *Arbeit macht frei* ("Work Sets You Free"). Notice the clock stopped at the time of liberation. In 1938, 50 inmates from another camp (Esterwegen) were transferred here for the purpose of building barracks; 900 more were transferred a few months later to build this concentration camp. Many of these inmates died during the construction of the camp.

In the fall of 1938, the camp opened. Most of the initial inmates were either Jews or communists. After "Crystal Night" (*Kristallnacht*) on vember 9, 1938, when Jewish businesses, synagogues and homes were attacked by Nazi mobs, 1,800 Jews were rounded up and placed here. Most were killed in the following weeks. By the fall of 1939, there were over 11,000 prisoners here. A typhus epidemic took the lives of many. In April of 1940, the first crematory was built. Shootings, hangings and torture became daily occurrences.

In January of 1942, inmates were forced to build "Station Z." Here, the first experiments of mass murder were made. In March of 1943, a gas chamber was added to Station Z. As the Allies advanced, 33,000 prisoners were forced to leave the camp on a Death March to the sea (where plans were to load the prisoners into boats and sink them). Thousands died during the Death March. The Soviet Army liberated the camp on April 22, 1945. Only 3,000 survived. After the war, it was used by the Russian secret police for the detention of criminals and others found to be undesirable by the GDR. Mass graves were found containing the remains of as many as 10,000 prisoners. It's estimated that 30,000-35,000 people lost their lives here. Sadly, there was an anti-Semitic arson attack here as recently as 1992. A grim and moving excursion.

Potsdam

To get to Potsdam from Berlin via the S-Bahn, take the S1 line to Potsdam Hauptbahnhof. It's about a 40-minute trip. Make sure you buy a ticket that includes zones "ABC."
Tel. 0331/275-5820 (tourist information)
The tourist-information center near the Potsdam S-Bahn station offers an English-speaking tour of the major sights (including the inside of the palace) for €26.
www.potsdam.de

Potsdam is best known for the Potsdam Conference held here in July and August of 1945. The "Big Three" leaders (U.S. President Truman, British Prime Minister Churchill and Soviet Premier Stalin) met to decide the fate of postwar Germany and Europe. It's a wonderful day-trip from Berlin, and its royal palace and park is Germany's version of France's Versailles. Within walking distance of the train station is the center of town, with some excellent examples of Prussian architecture (and some pretty horrid 1960s and 1970s buildings, as Potsdam was heavily bombed in World War II). Look for the massive dome when you exit the station and head toward it. Pick up a map (€3) at the tourist office along the main street (5 Friedrich-Ebert-Strasse) off of the train station. Here you'll find an **Egyptian obelisk** in front of the restored **Nikolaikirche** (St. Nicholas Church) with its massive dome. That building with Atlas on top of it is the **Altes Rathaus** (Old Town Hall), dating back to the mid-1750s. Its round tower was formerly a prison and is now a center for the arts.

Farther up Friedrich-Ebert-Strasse is the **Holländisches Viertel** (Dutch Quarter) in the area around Friedrich-Ebert-Strasse and Gutenbergstrasse (especially Mittelstrasse). Wander around and admire this collection of gabled buildings built in the 1730s. The area is filled with shops and restaurants.

Farther up Friedrich-Ebert-Strasse through the **Nauener Tor** (the castle-like city gate) and past (on your left) the **Stadthaus** (City Hall) will take you to **Alexandrowka**, a Russian settlement of wooden buildings dating back to the early 1800s, including a Russian Orthodox Church complete with onion dome. Potsdam's sister city in the United States is Sioux Falls, South Dakota. Now, talk about two different cities!

Schloss Sanssouci
(Sanssouci Palace)
Park Sanssouci
Tel. 0331/ 9694190
Open Apr-Oct Tues-Sun 9am-5pm, Nov-Mar Tues-Sun 9am-4pm
Admission: €8 (visits by guided tour only)

Surrounded by the one-square-mile Sanssouci Park (admission to the park is free), this summer palace was completed in 1747 for Frederick the Great who entertained the likes of French philosopher and writer Voltaire here. Surrounding the summer palace are terraces and landscaped gardens. It's one of Germany's most visited tourists attractions (so, keep that in mind and arrive early in the day). It's done in the rococo style and its grand Marble Hall will impress, as will the over-the-top music salon. In French, the name of the palace means "without a care" and Frederick was certainly enamored with

VISITING THE PARK SANS SOUCI

Opening hours vary for each building, but they're generally 9 or 10 a.m.-4 or 5 p.m., with shorter hours in the winter. To see the entire park, you'll need a full day. Many sights require a guided tour (in German with English pamphlet). From the Potsdam train station, take Bus 695. This bus has many stops throughout the park. Your U- and S-Bahn ticket for zones ABC allows you use of public transportation in Potsdam. The park's visitor's center is near the Windmühle (Windmill) west of Schloss Sanssouci. *Tel. 0331/9694202.*

Completed in 1864, this structure was built in the Italian Renaissance style to shelter plants during the winter. Today, it shelters 47 copies of paintings by Raphael.

Restaurant Tip:
Café und Restaurant Drachenhaus
Am Drachenberg (above the Orangerie)/4a Maulbeerallee
Tel. 0331/5053808
Open Mar-Oct 11am-7pm, Nov-Feb. Tues-Sun 11am-6pm
www.drachenhaus.de

Tired of looking at all those palaces? Take a break in the café located in the Dragon House, a Chinese pagoda named after the gargoyles on this building. Dine indoors, or out on the terraces. Moderate.

everything French. For an extra €2 you can take a guided tour of the nearby **Neue Kammern** (New Chambers), built to house the royal family's guests.

Orangerie
(Orangery)
Park Sanssouci/Maulbeerallee
Tel. 0331/9694280
Open May 15 to Oct 15 Tues-Sun 10am-5pm
Admission: €3 (with guide), €1 (without guide)

Bildergalerie
(Picture Gallery)
Park Sanssouci
Open mid-May to mid-Oct Tues-Sun 10am-5pm
Admission: €2

This building houses Frederick the Great's extensive collection of 17th-century Dutch, Flemish and Italian paintings. You might not pay attention to the paintings, as the elaborately decorated interior is a work of art in itself.

Neues Palais
(New Palace)
Park Sanssouci
Tel. 0331/9694255
Open Apr-Oct. Sat-Thur 9am-5pm, Nov-Mar Sat-Thur 9am- 4pm
Admission: €6 (with guide), €5 (without guide), €5 extra to see the King's apartments
www.spsg.de

Okay, it's not so new. Completed in 1769, the new palace is the largest structure in the park and has over 400 rooms. You can't miss its huge dome, and inside it's another rococo wonder filled antiques and 17th-century paintings. The Hall of Shells is an incredible room where the walls are covered with coral, seashells and semiprecious stones.

Neuer Garten
(New Garden)
On Heiliger See, 1 mile (.6 km) northwest of the palace
Tel. 0331/9694200
Open Apr-Oct Tues-Sun 9am-5pm, Nov-Mar Tues-Sun 9am-4pm
Admission: Free

Exceptionally maintained and beautiful gardens on **Heiliger See** (Holy Lake) one mile northwest of Park Sanssouci. Along the lake is the charming **Marmorpalais** (Marble Palace) *Admission: €3 (with guide), €2 (without guide)*

Schloss Cecilienhof
(Cecilienhof Palace)
In Neuer Garten (reached via tram or bus to Neuer Garten station)
Tel. 0331/9694244
Open Apr-Oct Tues-Sun 9am-5pm, Nov-Mar Tues-Sun 9am-4pm
Admission: €5 (with guide), €4 (without guide)
www.spsg.de

It was here at the famous Potsdam Conference in 1945 where the fates of postwar Germany and Europe were decided. You can visit the room where the declaration was signed. The palace built by Kaiser Wilhelm II (for Crown Prince Wilhelm) and completed in 1917 looks like an English manor house. Today, 45 of the building's 175 rooms are guest rooms of a luxury hotel. You can take guided tours of the prince's apartments at 11 a.m. and 2 p.m. Nearby, on a hill west of the palace, is **Belvedere auf dem Pfingstberg**, built as an observation platform for the royal family.

Schloss Charlottenhof
(Charlottenhof Palace)
South part of Park Sanssouci
Tel. 0331/9694228
Open mid-May to mid-Oct Tues-Sun 10am-5pm
Admission: €4 (guided tours only)

This Roman-style palace was completed in 1829. It was built by Friedrich Wilhelm IV, and has a remarkable blue entrance hall. You can also visit the **Römische Bäder** (Roman Baths), which were not built in Roman times, but in the 1830s. *Admission: €3 (with guide), €2 (without guide)*

Chinesisches Teehaus
(Chinese Teahouse)
Park Sanssouci
Tel. 0331/9694222
Open mid-May to mid-Oct Tues-Sun 10am-5pm
Admission: €1

The Chinese-style teahouse dates back to 1757 and is loaded with Chinese and Meissen porcelain.

Friedenskirche
(Peace Church)
Park Sanssouci
Tel. 0331/9694222
Open daily mid-May to mid-Oct.
Admission: Free

This Italianate church dates back to the mid-1800s and is known for its 12th-century mosaic.

2. WALKS

Berlin Wall Walking Tour

Note: for more detailed information on the sights in these walks, see the entries in chapter 1.

Highlights: **Brandenburger Tor**, **Potsdamer Platz**, **Kulturforum** and **Checkpoint Charlie**. Distance: Approximately one-and-a-half miles.

Between 1949 and 1961, three million people left East Berlin and East Germany. To stop this mass exodus, a 100-mile wall was built, a barrier that remained for 28 years. The wall was 13 feet tall and had a buffer zone of between 25 and 160 feet. Ultimately, 300 guard towers were built to monitor the area near the wall. In that 28-year period, 5,043 people are known to have successfully gotten around the wall. Guards fired at 1,693 people and made 3,221 arrests. Did you know that the East Germans referred to the wall as "The Anti-Fascist Protective Rampart"? Although most of the wall is gone today, this walk takes you along a portion of the former wall.

We start our walk at the Unter den Linden S-Bahn stop. Head down (west) on Unter den Linden toward the triumphal arch, the Brandenburger Tor. We'll take a walk east down Unter den Linden on the East Berlin Walking Tour (later in this book).

The square in front of the triumphal arch is **Pariser Platz**. The name of this square "celebrates" the German occupation of Paris in 1814. This was ground zero for bombing by the Allies in World War II. Today, it's lined with banks, hotels, German governmental offices and embassies, including, ironically, the French Embassy. You'll also find the British Embassy at 70 Wilhelmstrasse (just around the corner from the square).

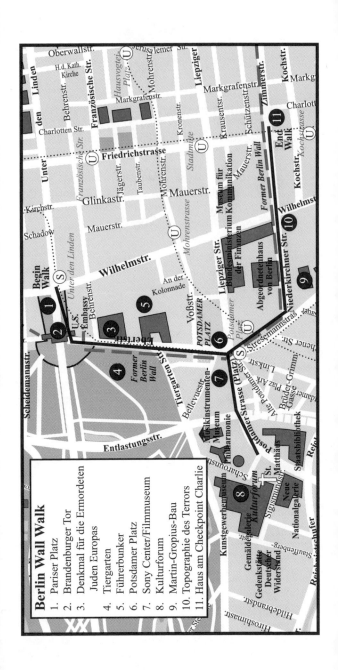

Berlin Wall Walk
1. Pariser Platz
2. Brandenburger Tor
3. Denkmal für die Ermordeten Juden Europas
4. Tiergarten
5. Führerbunker
6. Potsdamer Platz
7. Sony Center/Filmmuseum
8. Kulturforum
9. Martin-Gropius-Bau
10. Topographie des Terrors
11. Haus am Checkpoint Charlie

The very fancy Adlon Hotel is also here.

Now, head toward the triumphal arch.

The **Brandenburger Tor** (Brandenburg Gate) is probably Berlin's most recognizable sight. This famous gate was originally called the "Friedenstor" ("Gate of Peace"). Built in 1791 as a triumphal arch, it was at one time one of 18 gates in the capital of Prussia. The gate (pictured on the front of this book) features six Doric columns topped by the statue of Victory driving a four-horse chariot (it's facing toward you). The current statue is a copy dating back to 1958. The gate was the backdrop of many Nazi propaganda films. Badly damaged in World War II bombing, it was long in a sort of no man's land when the Berlin wall stood. When the wall came down, it was the sight of huge celebrations. It's recently been restored.

Head to the room built into the guard station (to the right as you face the gate).

The **Raum der Stille** (Room of Silence) allows you to quietly contemplate Berlin's turbulent history. It's meant to remind people of the original idea of the gate as a gate of peace.

Walk through the gate (with the Pariser Platz to your back)

In the distance, you can see the **Siegessäule** (Victory Column). We'll visit it on the West Berlin Walking Tour later in this book.

Now, turn left down Ebertstrasse to our next sight. You are now walking along the former Berlin Wall. You'll notice along this walk that the location of the former Berlin Wall is marked by a path of bricks set into the street.

On your left, just south of the Brandenburg Gate, is the construction site of the new **U.S. Embassy**.

Continue down the street. Our next sight is also to your left.

The **Denkmal für die Ermordeten Juden Europas** (Memorial to the Murdered European Jews) is a massive memorial of 2,700 pillars honoring Jews killed by the Nazis. Truly an impressive and thought-provoking memorial. You can also visit its underground center with information on the Holocaust.

Continue down Ebertstrasse.

To your right is the **Tiergarten**, Berlin's great green space right in the middle of the city.

As you continue down Ebertstrasse, to your left is a "sight" that will cause you to pause and reflect.

The location of the **Führerbunker** (Hitler's Bunker) is not marked by any signs, and the German government has specifically left it unmarked in fear that it would become a pilgrimage shrine for neo-Nazis. There's a children's playground on the spot where it's said that the bodies of Eva Braun and Adolph Hitler were burnt. Some of the bunker was destroyed by the Soviets at the end of the war, and other parts were recently discovered during a construction project.

A little farther down the street on your left is the **Berlin Hi-Flyer** (across from the Marriott Hotel) where you can view the sights in a hot air balloon (20).

Head to the large square at the end of Ebertstrasse.

Bombed beyond recognition in World War II, this square, **Potsdamer Platz**, found itself in East Berlin. Unused and undeveloped while the city was divided, after reunification, it became a huge construction site.

On the right side of the street at the intersection with Potsdamer Platz is a piece of the Berlin Wall. You'll see people taking photographs here.

Turn right at Potsdamer Platz (the sign says Potsdamer Platz, but this is also Potsdamer Strasse).

Soon on your right, you'll see the entrance for the **Sony Center**, a steel-and-glass entertainment complex that is home to tons of movie theaters, a dancing fountain, cafés and restaurants. The huge canopy (interestingly lit at night) is fantastic. This is also the location of the **Filmmuseum Berlin** (closed Mondays), devoted to the history of German film. Even if you're not a film buff, you'll find much of interest here.

After you've visited the Sony

Center, exit where you came in and turn right. You're now on Potsdamer Strasse. You'll soon be at our next stop.

The **Kulturforum** is home to the following:
- **Philharmonie**: Home of the Berlin Philharmonic Orchestra.
- **Staatsbibliothek**: The State Library.
- **Gemäldegalerie** (Picture Gallery): One of the world's greatest collections of European art from the 13th to the 18th century.
- **Neue Nationalgalerie** (New National Gallery): Filled with works by 20th-century German and international artists.
- **Kunstgewerbemuseum** (Museum of Arts and Crafts): Arts and crafts from the past 1,000 years are on display here.
- **Musikinstrumenten-Museum** (Musical Instruments Museum): Filled with every imaginable musical instrument. For more information on these sights, see the Potsdamer Platz section of this book.

After visiting the Sony Center and the Kulturforum, head back to the intersection of Ebertstrasse and Potsdamer Platz. Follow Stresemannstrasse (to your right) and turn left onto Niederkirchnerstrasse.

To your right at number 7 is **Martin-Gropius-Bau**. Built in 1881, this beautiful renovated building features changing art exhibits.

Directly across the street is the **Abgeordnetenhaus von Berlin**, a building dating back to the 1890s. It was the former Prussian parliament building, and now is home to the Berlin House of Deputies.

You can see portions of the Berlin Wall running along this street (to your right). Behind this section of the Berlin Wall is our next sight.

The Prinz Albrecht Palais (the former headquarters of Hitler's Gestapo) once stood here. Today it's the **Topographie des Terrors** (Topography of Terror). There's an exhibit here on the history of Nazi terror.

On the left side of the street is the **Bundesministerium der Finanzen** (German Finance Ministry). This Nazi-era building and former home to the Nazi Air Force (Luftwaffe) survived World War II bombing. While part of communist East Germany, it housed the Ministry of Ministries (no kidding)!

Continue down the street (the name of the street changes to Zimmerstrasse when you pass Wilhelmstrasse).

To your left at the corner of Friedrichstrasse and Zimmerstrasse is a memorial of crosses with the names of those killed attempting to flee East Berlin.

Our final stop is to your right at Friedrichstrasse (the street after Wilhelmstrasse).

Haus am Checkpoint Charlie (Checkpoint Charlie) at 43-45 Friedrichstrasse was the only checkpoint through which foreigners could pass between East and West Berlin. The history of the construction of the Berlin Wall is documented, along with incredible attempts to escape East Berlin. The checkpoint gets its name from checkpoint number three (as in the military code of Alpha for one, Bravo for two and Charlie for three). Some of the ways that people were smuggled into West Berlin are on display and they're very interesting. Attempts to escape included tunnels, hot-air balloons, a mini-submarine, cars and shopping carts! There's also a display dedicated to the Berlin Wall's demise in the 1989 peaceful revolution.

Our walk ends here. Note that if you continue north up Friedrichstrasse to the Stadtmitte U-Bahn stop, you can begin the next walk (or end this walk and return to your hotel).

Gendarmenmarkt Walking Tour

Highlights: **Konzerthaus, Französischer Dom, Deutscher Dom,** and **Nikolaiviertel**. Distance: Approximately one mile.

Take the U-Bahn to Stadtmitte. You'll begin your walk on Friedrichstrasse (at the intersection of Kronenstrasse). Head north on Friedrichstrasse.

You'll pass boutiques and stores along Friedrichstrasse. Stop at number 67 for some great chocolates and tarts at **Leysieffer**.

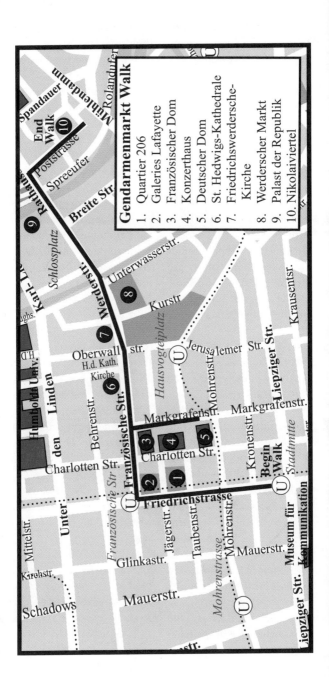

Gendarmenmarkt Walk

1. Quartier 206
2. Galeries Lafayette
3. Französischer Dom
4. Konzerthaus
5. Deutscher Dom
6. St. Hedwigs-Kathedrale
7. Friedrichswerdersche-Kirche
8. Werderscher Markt
9. Palast der Republik
10. Nikolaiviertel

After you pass Taubenstrasse, on your right on Friedrichstrasse are two department stores.

At number 71 is **Quartier 206**, selling all sorts of upscale goods. At number 75-78 (on the corner of Französische Strasse) is the Berlin branch of the famous French department store **Galeries Lafayette**. Don't miss the basement food market filled with French wines, breads, cheese and other French delicacies! Both stores are closed on Sundays. Underground shopping galleries connect them.

Turn right on Französische Strasse. After Charlottenstrasse, take a right at Markgrafenstrasse. You're now at the Gendarmenmarkt.

The **Gendarmenmarkt** is one of the most beautiful squares in Germany and all of Europe. It was created at the end of the 17th century as the Linden Markt, a marketplace. It gets its name from the Regiment Gens d'Armes who had their stables here in the 1770s. In the center of the square is a statue of Friedrich Schiller, the famous German poet. Three landmark buildings, the **Konzerthaus**, **Französischer Dom**, and **Deutscher Dom**, surround it.

The **Französischer Dom** (French Cathedral) is the home of the **Hugenottenmuseum**, which tells the story of the Huguenots, Protestants who arrived in Berlin after being expelled from France in the late 1600s. The tower offers picturesque views of the city (closed Mondays).

Between the two cathedrals is the **Konzerthaus** (Concert House), home to the famous Berlin and German Symphony orchestras. The building has been restored to its original 1821 glory, and has a grand staircase.

Also on Gendarmenmarkt is **Deutscher Dom** (German Cathedral) (closed Mondays). This church was built in the 1780s and is topped with a 23-foot-tall statue of Virtue. It's now the home of an exhibit called "Questions on German History."

There are lots of cafés here where you can take a break.

Head back to Französische Strasse and turn right. As you head up the street, you can see the grand Humboldt University in the distance to your left. It's located on Unter den Linden and is visited on the East Berlin Walking Tour later in this book. You'll soon find Hinter der Katholischen Kirche on your left. Turn left here and you'll soon be at our next sight.

St. Hedwigs-Kathedrale (St. Hedwig Cathedral) is the diocesan church of the Archdiocese of Berlin. It was completed in 1773 and modeled after the Pantheon in Rome. Its modern interior is a result of renovations by the GDR. Inside is a Madonna from the 16th century.

Return to Französische Strasse and continue down the street. At Niederlagstrasse is another church on your left.

The **Friedrichswerdersche-Kirche** (closed Mondays) was built in 1820 and rehabilitated in the 1980s. It's no longer used for religious services, and now houses a museum dedicated to Berlin's most influential architect Karl Schinkel and his works.

The street turns into Werderstrasse.

On your right, you'll pass the **Werderscher Markt**, the home of the German foreign ministry.

You'll cross one branch of the Spree River. You're now on Museumsinsel (Museum Island), in the Spree River.

On your left at Schlossplatz is the **Palast der Republik** (Palace of the Republic). This building is the former home of the parliament of the German Democratic Republic. It's been abandoned since the fall of the Berlin Wall (perhaps because it's so unattractive). Will it still be standing by the time you read this? Who knows, as it's scheduled for demolition.

Cross the other branch of the Spree River and the street turns into Rathausstrasse. Pass the river walk Spreeufer and turn right onto Poststrasse.

Note that if you continue straight on Rathausstrasse, you'll run into Alexanderplatz. For information on the sights around Alexanderplatz (and that huge television tower rising above it), check out the East Berlin Walking Tour and the Alexanderplatz chapter of this book.

You're now in the **Nikolaiviertel** (Nicholas Quarter). Named after the St. Nicholas Church, this quarter of Berlin is its oldest. The East German government painstakingly reconstructed the remains of medieval and baroque buildings. Among the highlights are the **Ephraim-Palais** (16 Poststrasse) with its rococo balcony, and the **Knoblauch-Haus** (23 Poststrasse), both of which you can visit to see their grand interiors. The **Nikolaikirche** (St. Nicholas Church) (also on Poststrasse) is Berlin's oldest church, dating back to the 14th century. You can visit an exhibit of archeological finds that tells the history of Berlin until the 1600s. Photographs show the wartime destruction and reconstruction of the church.

There are plenty of restaurants and cafés here, especially on Spreeufer along the river, where you can end your walk. There are also lots of souvenir shops, some with unique relics from the GDR past.

To return to your hotel, you can head to either the Klosterstrasse or Alexanderplatz U-Bahn stops.

East Berlin Walking Tour

Highlights: **Unter den Linden**, **Museumsinsel**, and **Alexanderplatz**. Distance: Approximately one-and-a-half miles.

We start our walk at the Unter den Linden S-Bahn stop. Exit out of the S-Bahn stop by following the signs for "Russische Botschaft."

The famous boulevard **Unter den Linden** got its name from the linden trees that line it. When the Berlin Wall divided the city, this street was in East Berlin. Once again, it has become one of Europe's grand boulevards.

*Walk toward the tall television tower (heading east) with the triumphal arch, the **Brandenburg Gate**, to your back. Head down the right side of the street.*

Just past Wilhelmstrasse is our first sight.

You can't miss the huge Stalinist 1950s building at number 63-65 on the right side of the street. The **Russische Botschaft** Russian

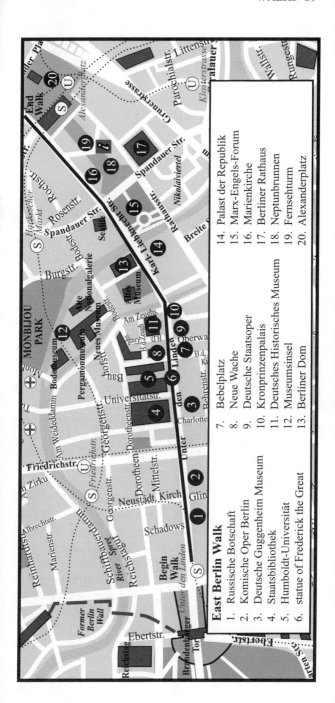

East Berlin Walk

1. Russische Botschaft
2. Komische Oper Berlin
3. Deutsche Guggenheim Museum
4. Staatsbibliothek
5. Humboldt-Universität
6. statue of Frederick the Great
7. Bebelplatz
8. Neue Wache
9. Deutsche Staatsoper
10. Kronprinzenpalais
11. Deutsches Historisches Museum
12. Museumsinsel
13. Berliner Dom
14. Palast der Republik
15. Marx-Engels-Forum
16. Marienkirche
17. Berliner Rathaus
18. Neptunbrunnen
19. Fernsehturm
20. Alexanderplatz

Embassy) was one of the first large postwar construction projects in East Berlin. It's built in the style known as "Zuckerbäckerstil" or "wedding cake-style," and you'll understand why when you see it. Notice the hammer-and-sickle in the cement work above the windows.

Continue down Unter den Linden and pass Glinkastrasse.

At number 41 is the **Komische Oper Berlin** (Comic Opera Berlin). Musical theater, ballet and opera performances are held here. The original baroque interior survives, but the exterior is from the 1960s. Also here is the **Kunstsalon**, a strange and interesting shop selling souvenirs and leftovers from opera productions. You'll find everything from stage props to costumes.

As you're walking along this street, you'll see those silly men on traffic lights. They're called **Ampelmännchen** and they're a leftover of communist rule. They're so popular that there was an outcry when many were being replaced by modern traffic lights. You'll see shops selling souvenirs with the little men

on them throughout the city. By the way, Germans don't jaywalk!

Pass Friedrichstrasse and Charlottenstrasse.

On the corner of Charlottenstrasse at number 15 is the **Deutsche Guggenheim Berlin** (German Guggenheim Museum), located on the ground floor of the Berlin headquarters of Deutsche Bank. This is one of the famous Guggenheim Museums of contemporary and modern art. You'll find changing exhibits and an emphasis on avant-garde German artists.

On the left side of the street is the grand **Staatsbibliothek** (State Library) at number 8. It has a lovely courtyard. Next door is the **Humboldt-Universität zu Berlin** (Humboldt University of Berlin) at number 6. Statues of the founders, the brothers Humboldt, are featured prominently on the superb façade of this grand university. Albert Einstein taught here and Karl Marx was a student. It's often the site of an outdoor book market.

In the center of Unter den Linden is a statue of Frederick the Great on his horse. He was King of Prussia from 1740 to 1786, and one of the most famous German rulers of all time for both his military successes and his domestic reforms that made Prussia one of the leading European nations.

The square across from the Humboldt University (on the right side of the street) is our next sight.

It was here at **Bebelplatz** (Bebel Square) on May 10, 1933, that the Nazis had their infamous book burning. A memorial set into the middle of the square commemorates this event. There's a glass floor where you can see a large underground room with empty shelves symbolizing the 25,000 books by "enemies" of the government that were burned here. Access to the memorial will resume after construction in the area is completed.

At the corner of Oberwallstrasse (on the left side of the street) is our next sight.

The **Neue Wache** (New Guard House) is a former guard house dating back to 1816. It's now the site of a memorial to the victims of war and tyranny. The remains of both the unknown soldier and unknown concentration camp victims are here surrounded by soil gathered from World War II, concentration camps and battlefields. Head inside (admission free) to see the moving statue by Käthe Kollwitz, *Mother With Her Dead Son*.

On the right side of the street are these sights.

At number 5-7 is the **Deutsche Staatsoper** (German State Opera). The original building was destroyed in World War II and the copy you see today was built in 1955. Locals call it Staatsoper Unter den Linden. This is the home of the German State Opera, an opera company that traces its roots back to the 1700s. If you attend an event, the lavish interior with immense chandeliers and ornate walls will impress. The beautiful **Operncafe** is here.

Next door at number 3 is the **Kronprinzenpalais** (Crown Prince's Palace), former home of Frederick the Great. The building is a re-creation of the former palace (the old one was bombed). It served as the guesthouse for dignitaries visiting the GDR. It was here that the agreement to unify Germany were signed on August 31, 1990.

At number 2 (on the left side just before the Spree River) is our next sight.

The **Deutsches Historisches Museum** (German History Museum) is housed in a former armory (the Zeughaus) and has a new wing designed by IM Pei (who designed the glass pyramid at the Louvre in Paris). Period rooms tell the history of Germany through changing exhibits.

*Cross the Spree River and you are now on **Museumsinsel** (Museum Island), in the Spree River. This was the original settlement of Berlin back in the 1200s.*

To your left are several museums:
•**Altes Museum** (Old Museum): Contains a collection of Roman and Greek antiquities and is the temporary home of the Egyptian Museum.
•**Pergamonmuseum**: One of the world's largest museums of archeology.
•**Alte Nationalgalerie** (Old National Gallery): Home to Germany's largest collection of 19th-century art and sculpture.
•**Neues Museum** (New Museum): Will eventually house the Egyptian Museum and the Primeval and Early History Museum.
•**Bode Museum**: Will ultimately house the Museum of Byzantine Art, Collection of Antique Sculpture and Coin Cabinet.

You can learn more about these museums in the Museumsinsel section of this book.

On your left side before you leave the island by (again) crossing over the Spree River is our next sight.

The **Berliner Dom** (Berlin Cathedral) dates back to the early 1900s. A church has been on this site for centuries. It was heavily bombed in World War II and remained mostly in ruins until renovation began in the 1970s. Today, the interior of this Italian Renaissance-style cathedral has been restored to its former, and very ornate, glory. Its crypt contains the remains of the House of Hohenzollern, the Prussian rulers from 1701-1918. The panoramic views of the city from the dome are beyond compare. Hope you like to climb steps, as there are 270 of them.

That huge, ugly 1970s building on your right is the **Palast der Republik** (Palace of the Republic), the former home of the German Democratic Republic (East Germany). It's scheduled for demolition.

Cross the Spree River (again) and the street turns into Karl-Liebknecht-Strasse. Continue down Karl-Liebknecht-Strasse.

You'll pass the large square **Marx-Engels-Forum** on your right with bigger-than-life statues of Karl Marx and Friedrich Engels along with photographs etched in stainless-steel pillars featuring the struggles of the world's workers. Hop into their laps and have your photo taken!

Continue down Karl-Liebknecht-Strasse. Just after the Radisson Hotel at number 5, step into the covered courtyard to your left. Walk down about half way until you see a blue frosted door on your left. Enter the café inside and walk straight to the elevator in front of you. Look up at our next sight.

In the atrium of the Radisson Hotel is an amazing 82-foot-tall aquarium. It's part of **Sealife Berlin**.

Return to Karl-Liebknecht-Strasse and continue walking until you cross Spandauer Strasse.

At number 8 (on your right) is **Marienkirche** (St. Mary's Church). Parts of this Gothic church date back to 1270. Of note are the baroque pulpit made of marble and the ornate 18th-century organ. Right inside the door is a mysterious painting dating back to 1475 named *The Dance of Death*. It was discovered under a layer of white paint in 1860.

That red brick building across the square is the **Berliner Rathaus** (Berlin City Hall), built in 1860. The stonework on the front of the building tells the history of Berlin. The magnificent fountain here is the **Neptunbrunnen** (Neptune Fountain).

Continue down Karl-Liebknecht-Strasse toward the huge tower.

A television tower, the **Fernsehturm**, dominates the area. You can take the elevator up to the observation deck at the top for great views. You can also have a snack at the revolving café/restaurant.

Continue down Karl-Liebknecht-Strasse toward our last sight.

The East German government developed this huge square, **Alexanderplatz**, in the 1970s and you can tell! You'll find hideous communist-era buildings along with a silly-looking clock, the **Weltzeituhr** (World Clock), with an atom design on top telling you the time in such important communist strongholds as Havana and Hanoi. The graffiti-covered fountain on the square has a wonderfully communist name: **Brunner der Völkerfreundschaft** or "Fountain of the Friendship of Peoples."

You end your walk here. You can return to your hotel by using the Alexanderplatz S- and U-Bahn stops.

West Berlin Walking Tour

Highlights: Kaiser-Wilhelm Gedächtniskirche, Tiergarten and the **Reichstag**. Distance: Over two miles.

Take the U-Bahn to the Kurfürstendamm stop. We'll begin our walk along Kurfürstendamm (known as Ku'damm). This is the main shopping street of what used to be West Berlin.

Head for the interesting ruins of the **Kaiser-Wilhelm Gedächtniskirche** (Kaiser Wilhelm Memorial Church). Allied bombs in the last days of World War II demolished all but a few walls and the tower of the Kaiser Wilhelm church, which had stood here since the late 1800s. It's a moving reminder of the destruction this city has seen. In 1961, a new octagonal-shaped church was built into the ruins. There are 11,000 blue windows in the annex. The free museum here tells the story of the old church, the bombing of the church and surrounding areas, and the phoenix of the new church.

Walk up the street toward the building with the Mercedes

Benz symbol on top. The street curves right off of Ku'damm and becomes Tauentzienstrasse.

The 22-story **Europa-Center** (the one with the Mercedes Benz symbol on top) has shops, bars, restaurants, movie theaters and clubs. There are great views from the observation deck. The Center is located on Breitscheidplatz. You can take a break and watch the street performers here around the red-granite **Weltenbrunnen** (World Fountain) that features a world split open.

As you walk down Tauentzienstrasse, you'll see the sculpture Berlin in the center of the street. It's meant to symbolize the city. Placed there before the city was reunited, the tubes intertwine, but never connect, representing life in the city before reunification.

Head straight to 21-24 Tauentzienstrasse (on the right side of the street) to the large KaDeWe department store.

On the sixth floor of the **KaDeWe (Kaufhaus des Westens)** department store is the largest food hall in Europe. There are over thirty places to eat. German regional specialties can be found at all prices. You can sample over 1,300 types of cheese, 1,200 sausages and cold cuts, 240 desserts, 400 types of bread and rolls and 2,400 wines from five continents. If you can't find something you like here, you're really picky! It's closed on Sundays.

Return to the corner of Tauentzienstrasse and Nürnberger Strasse. Turn right onto Nürnberger Strasse. Cross Kurfürstenstrasse and the square Olof-Palme-Platz.

Across the square (to your left) is the Aquarium of the **Zoologischer Garten Berlin** (Berlin Zoo). Berlin's oldest zoo also has a huge aviary– and giant pandas!

When you cross the square, you'll be on Budapester Strasse. Walk along this street for a while past the hotels, including the Intercontinental Hotel. The street becomes Stülerstrasse when you cross the canal **Landwehrkanal.**

Now that Berlin is once again the capital of Germany, countries are reestablishing their embassies here, especially in this area. That green copper building to your right is the **Scandinavian Embassies Complex.**

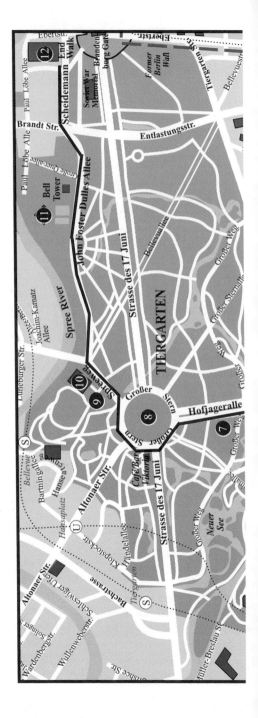

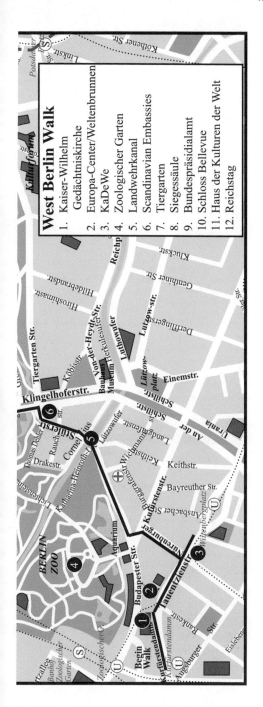

West Berlin Walk

1. Kaiser-Wilhelm Gedächtniskirche
2. Europa-Center/Weltenbrunnen
3. KaDeWe
4. Zoologischer Garten
5. Landwehrkanal
6. Scandinavian Embassies
7. Tiergarten
8. Siegessäule
9. Bundespräsidialamt
10. Schloss Bellevue
11. Haus der Kulturen der Welt
12. Reichstag

Turn left onto Klingelhöferstrasse/ Hofjägerallee and you'll enter our next sight.

The **Tiergarten** is a huge 412-acre park in the middle of the city. It was opened to the public in the 1700s and is filled with walkers, runners and, in good weather, Berliners having picnickers and sunbathers.

Hofjägerallee leads to our next sight.

The **Siegessäule** (Victory Column) commemorates Prussian military victories against France, Austria and Denmark.

Turn to your left and cross the main street in the park Strasse

---

DETOUR

To reach the Victory Column, you can head through the tunnel contained in the building with the columns on it next to the café. The tunnel will take you under the busy street to the Column. In the monument, you can climb the spiral staircase to reach an observation platform with good views of the park and the surrounding area (€3).

---

des 17. Juni (named after the June 17, 1953 uprising in East Berlin that was crushed by the Soviets).

Now's a good time for a break at the **Café/Bar Viktoria** where you can have a snack and a drink.

Now, head to Spreeweg (one of the streets that veers off the intersection).

You'll see large statues of German rulers including Bismarck, the "Iron Chancellor." Under his rule, Germany grew from a loose confederation of weak states to a unified powerful empire.

The oval-shaped building on your left is the **Bundespräsidialamt**, where Germany's president has his offices. A little bit farther down on your left is the palace **Schloss Bellevue**, the home of the German president. If the president is there, the German flag will be flying from the flagpole on the roof.

Just after the palace, turn right onto John-Foster-Dulles-Allee (the sign is on the right side of the street). This street is named after the U.S. Secretary of State under the Eisenhower administration. He was a fervent anti-communist who saw Berlin on the frontline of communist expansion. After walking a bit along the Spree River, you'll pass (on your left) our next sight at number 10.

The "pregnant oyster" (as the locals call it) houses the **Haus der Kulturen der Welt** (House of World Cultures). Exhibits dedicated to world culture, from art to film, are held here. The building (formerly the Congress Hall or Kongresshalle) was a gift from the United States and opened in 1958. You'll also pass a modern **bell-tower.**

Continue down John-Foster-Dulles-Allee (it turns into Scheidemannstrasse). Those modern buildings to your left are part of the Bundeskanzleramt, the German Federal Chancellery. You're now facing our final sight.

The **Reichstag** is the seat of the German Parliament. It was constructed between 1884 and 1894. It's had a turbulent history. Fire broke out in the building in 1933, destroying most of it. It's believed that followers of Hitler started the fire, but the Com-munists were blamed. This infamous event allowed Hitler to round up and arrest "enemies" of the government. It was heavily damaged by Allied bombing, and when the Soviet Army entered the city at the end of World War II. It was not used from 1933 to 1999. The building took on new meaning after reunification, when Berlin was restored as the capital of Germany. Since April 1999, the Reichstag is again the seat of the Bundestag (the German parliament). Today's design is by British architect Sir Norman Foster, who added a fantastic glass dome. Light enters the dome and reflects off 360 mirrors in the dome. At night, the dome is lit from inside. The lobby features a huge 60-foot German flag. The dome can be reached by taking the elevator. You then walk up spiral ramps to the top (there's also a rooftop restaurant). Admission is free, and you'll most likely have to wait in line to enter.

You'll end your walking tour here. The closest S-Bahn stop (to return to your hotel) is the Unter den Linden stop.

Charlottenburg Walking Tour

Highlights: **Sammlung Berggruen, Schloss Charlottenburg** and **Schlossgarten Charlottenburg.** Distance: Less than one mile (excluding the gardens).

Note that most of the sights on this walk are closed on Mondays.

Take the U-Bahn to Sophie-Charlotte Platz where we will begin our walk. Head up (north) from this square on Schlossstrasse. You're heading straight for Schloss Charlottenburg.

To your right after Schustehrusstrasse and Wulfsheinstrasse are the **Schlossstrasse Villas.** These restored villas (especially at numbers 63, 65 and 67) give you an idea of what this area was like at the end of the 19th century when it was home to Berlin's wealthiest residents.

Also to your right at number 69b is **Abguss-Sammlung Antiker Plastik Berlin.** Classical-sculpture fans can view works spanning 3,500 years (open 2 p.m. to 5 p.m. Tuesday through Saturday, and noon to 5 p.m. on Sunday). At number 69 is **Heimatmuseum Charlottenburg-Wilmersdorf** (open 2 p.m. to 5 p.m. Thursday through Sunday). This local-history museum features changing exhibits.

Across the street at number 1a is our next museum.

The **Bröhan-Museum** contains a huge collection of Art Nouveau and Art Deco objects, paintings and furnishings. (German Art Nouveau is called "Jugendstil"). It's closed on Mondays.

Next door (also on your left) at number 1 is **Sammlung Berggruen: Picasso und Seine Zeit** (The Berggruen Collection: Picasso and His Era). This museum contains the private collection of Heinz Berggruen, an art dealer. The vast majority of the works here are by Picasso, such as his famous 1939 painting *Woman in a Hat.* The collection also contains works by such notables as van Gogh, Matisse, Klee and Cèzanne. It's closed on Mondays.

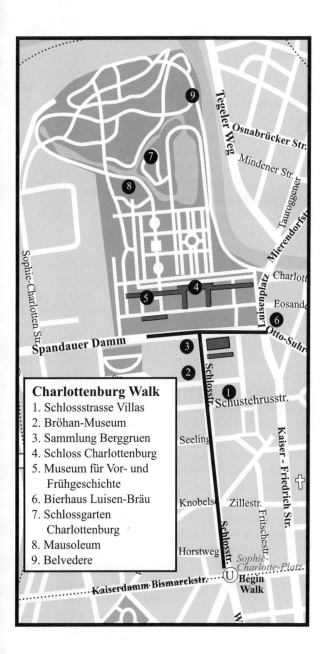

Charlottenburg Walk

1. Schlossstrasse Villas
2. Bröhan-Museum
3. Sammlung Berggruen
4. Schloss Charlottenburg
5. Museum für Vor- und
   Frühgeschichte
6. Bierhaus Luisen-Bräu
7. Schlossgarten
   Charlottenburg
8. Mausoleum
9. Belvedere

Straight ahead at the end of Schlossstrasse is our next sight.

The **Schloss Charlottenburg** was built by King Friedrich I in the late 1600s for his wife Sophie Charlotte as a summer residence. Over the years, additions by subsequent kings increased its size. Like so many other historic buildings in Berlin, it was severely damaged in World War II, but has been reconstructed. Notice the statue of King Friedrich on his horse as you enter. The apartments of the king and his wife in the **Altes Schloss** (Old Palace) include the over-the-top **Reception Chamber** lined with mirrored walls and tapestries dating back to the early 1700s, and the incredible collection of porcelain from China in the **Porcelain Chamber**. The **Neue Flügel** (New Wing), also known as the Knobelsdorff-Flügel, contains the apartments of Frederick the Great (Friedrich II) and the Hohenzollern-Museum, featuring a selection of items from the royal collection. The **Neue Pavillon** (New Pavilion) was constructed in 1825 as an Italianate villa. It houses an art museum.

To the left of Schloss Charlottenburg is another museum.

The **Museum für Vor- und Frühgeschichte** (Museum of Primeval and Early History) follows the evolution of man from 1,000,000 B.C. to the Bronze Age. You'll find everything from Stone-Age tools to finds from the ancient city of Troy. It's closed on Mondays.

Need a break? To the right of Schloss Charlottenburg as you face the palace is a traditional Berlin eatery.

Bierhaus Luisen-Bräu at 1 Luisenplatz isn't the place to go if you're looking for fine dining. But try this beer hall for it buffet table filled with hearty (some might say overly heavy) traditional German dishes, where there's indoor and outdoor dining at picnic tables, and the featured beverage is constantly flowing. It's inexpensive and a good place for a break, even if just for a beer.

Behind the Schloss Charlottenburg is our final stop.

You can wander the formal, huge gardens **Schlossgarten Charlottenburg**. They've been here since 1697. You'll see swans swimming in small lakes, the **Mausoleum** containing the remains of many members of the Prussian royal family, and **Belvedere**, the royal teahouse, with an extensive collection of 18th-century porcelain.

Take your time and enjoy this peaceful end to your walk. You can head back to the Sophie-Charlotte-Platz U-Bahn to return to your hotel.

3. MISCELLANY

Dining

Beyond the simple need to nourish oneself, dining in a foreign country gives you an insight into the soul of its people. It's a glimpse of their customs, their likes and dislikes, their foibles, their accomplishments. It puts you in contact with local culture.

Before you leave for Berlin, stop thinking in stereotypes. Be as liberal and accepting as the Berliners. Food in Germany is no longer just bratwurst, sauerkraut and beer. Oh, you'll find plenty of traditional heavy foods that will make you feel like a *Schwein* (pig), especially on hot summer days, but you'll also find innovative, light cuisine.

There's no need to spend a lot of money in Berlin to have good meal. There are all kinds of fabulous foods to be had inexpensively.

Eat at a neighborhood restau-rant. You'll usually know the price of a meal before entering, as almost all restaurants in Europe post the menu and prices in the window. Never order anything whose price is not known in advance.

Imbiss (snack stands) serve inexpensive sausages and snacks. Delis and food stores can provide cheap and wonderful meals. Buy some cheese, bread, wine and other snacks and have a picnic in one of Berlin's great parks. Remember to pack a corkscrew and eating utensils when you leave home. No corkscrew? Just buy a beer!

Lunch, even at the most expensive restaurants listed in this guide, always has a lower price. So, have lunch as your main meal.

Restaurants that have menus written in English (especially those near tourist attractions) are almost always more expensive than neighborhood restaurants.

If you are concerned about the cost of a meal, the *Tageskarte* (menu of the day) is usually a better value for your money than purchasing food *á la carte*.

Street vendors generally sell inexpensive and good food. For the cost of a cup of coffee or a drink, you can linger at a café and watch the world pass you by for as long as you want. It's one of Berlin's greatest bargains.

And don't eat at McDonald's or Burger King (there are now more than 1,000 in Germany), for God's sake.

Top Ten Rules for Dining in Berlin

1. Learn some basic German. We aren't suggesting that you take a course on German grammar. It's just common courtesy to greet people you meet in their own language. Although many Germans speak English, they greatly appreciate any effort to speak their language.

2. Avoid eating in a restaurant that has a menu written in English. It's usually a sign that the restaurant caters to tourists and you'll miss having an authentic German meal.

3. Don't be afraid to approach locals. They can't and won't hurt you. They are not laughing at you, they don't dislike you, they aren't even thinking about you.

4. Try to make reservations at a restaurant. This isn't as difficult as it seems; the words are similar in both languages and they'll get the gist of what you're trying to do. Do a walk-by in the afternoon and stop in to make the reservation.

5. Return to a restaurant if you like it. If you have the luxury of time and can resist the temptation to try other restaurants, you'll always be treated better if they recognize you. Few travelers return to the same restaurant.

6. Europeans dine leisurely. Don't expect to get the same speed of service as at home. For Germans, dining is an integral part of their day, a time to rest, relax and talk to their friends and family.

7. Don't talk loudly. Americans often speak loudly; we just can't help it. But believe us: Those loud voices, coupled with running shoes, backpacks, "fanny packs," conspicuous travel-guide books and cameras are like wearing a neon sign that says "I am an American tourist."

8. Stand your ground without being aggressive. In the years we've been traveling, it seems that waiters have become more relaxed about the rituals of eating, and will accommodate you if you insist on what you want—within reason, of course.

9. Visit a street vendor at least once. Whether it's sandwiches, or *Wurst* (sausage), vendors sell delicious "food on the run." Do yourself a favor, and sample some.

10. Always be courteous. Remember that you are a guest in their country.

Tipping

A service charge is almost always added to your bill (*Rechnung*) in Germany. Depending on the service, it's sometimes appropriate to leave a small tip. Germans usually round up 5-10%. So, if your meal costs €27, you can round up to €30. The menu will usually note that service is included (*mit Bedienung* or *Bedienung*

inbegriffen or *inklusive Bedienung*). Don't leave the tip on the table. It's considered rude. If you say "thanks" or *"danke"* when you give money to the waiter or waitress, they will likely not bring change back to you. Berliners will frequently tell the server exactly how much change they want returned. In bars and cafés, it's common to round up and leave the change.

Mealtimes

In Berlin, breakfast is served as early as 7 a.m., lunch is served from noon to around 2 p.m., and dinner is usually served from 7 p.m. to 10 p.m.

Water

Europeans joke that you can tell a U.S. tourist from his backpack, clothes and bottle of mineral water. Tap water is safe in Berlin, but remember that Berliners never ask for it in a restaurant. It's just unacceptable to them.

Restaurants in this Guide

Each of our recommended restaurants offers something different. Some have great food and little ambiance. Others have great ambiance and adequate food. Still others have both. Our goal is to find restaurants that are moderately priced and enjoyable.

RESTAURANT PRICES

Restaurant prices in this book are for a main course and without wine:

Inexpensive: under €10
Moderate: €11-20
Expensive: €21-30
Very Expensive: over €30

All restaurants have been tried and tested. Not enough can be said for a friendly welcome and great service. No matter how fabulous the meal, the experience will always be better when the staff treats you as if they actually want you there rather than simply tolerating your presence.

Menu Translator
Aal, eel
Apfel, apple
Apfelsine, orange
Austern, oysters
Banane, banana
Bier, beer
Bohnen, beans
Brot, bread
Brötchen, rolls
Eier, eggs
Eintritt, cover charge
Eintopf, stew
Ente, duck
Erbsen, peas
Erdbeere, strawberry
Erdnuss, peanut
Fasan, pheasant
Fisch, fish

Flasche, bottle
Fleisch, meat
Forelle, trout
Frühstück, breakfast
Gans, goose
Garnelen, shrimp
gebacken, baked
gebraten, fried
gedämpft, steamed
Geflügel, poultry
gegrillt, grilled
gekocht, boiled
Gemüse, vegetables
geräuchert, smoked
Glas, glass
Hähnchen (Huhn), chicken
heiss, hot
Hering, herring
Himbeere, raspberry
Hirsch, deer
Hummer, lobster
Jakobsmuscheln, scallops
Kabeljau, cod
Kaffee, coffee
Kalbfleisch, veal
kalt, cold
Kaninchen, rabbit
Kartoffel, potato
Käse, cheese
Kirsche, cherry
Knoblauch, garlic
Krabbe, crab
koffeinfrei, decaffeinated
Kohl, cabbage
Kopfsalat, lettuce
Lachs, salmon
Lamm, lamb
Lebel, liver
Mais, corn
Meeresfrüchte, seafood
Meerrettich, horseradish

Milch, milk
mit, with
Mohrrüben, carrots
Muscheln, mussels
Nachspeise, dessert
Nuss, nut
Obst, fruit
Pampelmuse, grapefruit
paniert, breaded
Paprika, pepper
Pilze, mushrooms
Pommes frites, french fries
Pute, turkey
Rechnung, check/bill
Reh, venison
Rind(er), beef
roh, raw
Saft, juice
Salat, salad
Salz, salt
Schinken, ham
Schokolade, chocolate
Schwein(e), pork
Spargel, asparagus
Speck, bacon
Speisekarte, menu
Spezialität, specialty
Suppe, soup
Süssstoff, artificial sweetener

LET'S DRINK!

beer, Bier (*beer*)
wine, Wein (*vine*)
red, rot (*roht*)
white, weiss (*vise*)
bottle, Flasche (***flah**-sheh*)
glass, Glas (*glahs*)
coffee, Kaffee (*kah-**fay***)
tea, Tee (*tay*)
more, mehr (*mehr*)
water, Wasser (*vah-ser*)
Cheers!, Prost! (*prohst*)

Taube, pigeon
Tee, tea
Tintenfisch, squid
Thunfisch, tuna
Tomaten, tomatoes
Truthahn, turkey
Vorspeisen, appetizers
Wachtel, quail
Wasser, water
Wein, wine
Weintrauben, grapes
Wurst, sausage
Zitrone, lemon
Zucker, sugar
Zwiebeln, onions

Airports & Getting Around

Airports/Arrival
There are three airports serving Berlin, and shuttle buses run frequently between all three. Most Northern Americans arrive through Tegel (5 miles [8 km] northwest of the central city). A taxi to the central city costs around €20 and takes 20 minutes (de-

pending on traffic). Buses (€2) run here (X9 and 109) to the Bahnhof Zoo (in the western part of the city) every 15 minutes, with stops at major U- and S-Bahn stations. Bus TXL goes to Alexanderplatz (in the eastern part of the city), with stops at major U-Bahn and S-Bahn stations. You can take public transportation from these stops to your hotel. There's a tourist-information booth in the main terminal that can help steer you in the right direction.

Many Eastern European, Russian and Asian flights use Schönefeld (12 miles [19 km] from the central city). A taxi costs about €40. S-Bahn (line 9) to the central city is a 45-minute ride (approximately €3).

Flights from other German cities (and some nearby European destinations) use Tempelhof (4 miles [6 km] southeast of the city center). Taxis cost approximately €20 to the central city. U-Bahn (Platz der Luftbrücke) or bus #109 run to the central city (approximately €3). Tempelhof's future is uncertain.

If you arrive by train at either Berlin Ostbahnhof or Bahnhof Zoologischer Garten, you can reach your final destination by taxi or S-Bahn connections. The new Lehrter Bahnhof, located conveniently in the central city, will open in 2006.

Cars and Driving
Are you crazy? Parking is chaotic, gas is extremely expensive, and driving in Berlin is an unpleasant "adventure" (although not nearly as chaotic as Paris or Rome). With the incredible public-transportation system, there's absolutely no reason to rent a car. If you drive to your hotel, park it and leave it there and use public transportation or your feet.

Here's how you convert kilometers to miles: 1 kilometer = .62 miles. To convert miles to kilometers, multiply by 1.61. So, one mile = 1.61 kilometers.

Public Transportation
Don't be afraid to use public transportation. Berlin's public-transportation network is easy to use. You can change from underground (U-Bahn) to surface rail (S-Bahn), to trams (in former East Berlin only) to bus with one ticket for two hours after validation. Berlin

is divided into transport zones A, B and C, but most visitors will only travel in zones A and B.

There are ticket-vending machines at each station with instructions in English. There is an office of the public-transportation system (the BVG) at the airport where you can buy your passes.

GET A TICKET!

You must have a validated ticket, so look for the validating machine before you get on. Officials (dressed in civilian clothes) do random spot checks. They'll whip out badges between stops. If you don't have a validated ticket, you're going to pay a significant fine (€40). Believe me, they do check!

Tickets and Travel Cards for AB (2 zones)/ABC (3 zones):

Single Ticket (*Einzelticket*): €2/€2.60. Valid for two hours with unlimited stops.

Short-Hop Ticket (*Kurzfahrstrecke*): €1.20. Valid for three U- or S-Bahn stops and six bus or tram stops.

Day Ticket (*Tageskarte*): €5.60/€6.00. Valid until 3a.m. of the day after validation.

7-Day-Ticket (*Wochenkarte*): €24.30/€30.00. Ticket is transferable and valid for 7 days after validation.

The *WelcomeCard* costs €16 (for two consecutive days) and €22 (for three consecutive days), and provides discounts to certain museums and tours and free public transportation within Berlin. It's available at tourist-information centers.

Budget Bus Tour

A good and inexpensive way to see many major sights in Berlin is to take bus #100 departing frequently from Bahnhof Zoologischer Garten (the "Zoo Station"). The one-way trip costs the price of a bus ticket (€2). You can get on and off as often as you like within two hours after your ticket is validated. The trip takes between 30 to 45 minutes (depending on traffic). Try to sit in the front on the upper level. Here are some of the sights you'll see:

•**Kaiser-Wilhelm Gedächtniskirche**
(Kaiser Wilhelm Memorial Church)

•**Kurfürstendamm**
(The former West Berlin's main street)
•**Zoologischer Garten Berlin**
(Berlin Zoo)
•**Tiergarten**
(Berlin's huge park in the center of the city)
•**Siegessäule**
(Victory Column)
•**Schloss Bellevue**
(Home of Germany's president)
•**Reichstag**
(The German parliament building)
•**Brandenburger Tor**
(Brandenburg Gate)
•**Pariser Platz**
(The square facing the Brandenburg Gate)
•**Unter den Linden**
(The former East Berlin's main street)
•**Deutsche Staatsoper**
(German State Opera)

•**Berliner Dom**
(Berlin Cathedral)
•**Alexanderplatz**
(The former East Berlin's huge square, dominated by the television tower)

Bike Rentals
A great way to see Berlin is to rent a bike. The DB, the German rail system, operates a bike rental in the summer. You'll see the bikes locked up at major tourist sights. You call the telephone number on the bike and give your credit-card information. You then get a code that allows you to open the lock. This same code will allow you to lock and unlock the bike. The rental cost is less than €2 per half-hour. When you've had enough, just call the telephone number again and you'll get a code to lock up the bike.

Berlin by Season

Here are a few annual events in Berlin. For a complete list of events being held during your visit, check out *www.berlin-tourist-information.de*.

Winter
•**W e i h n a c h t s m ä r k t e**
(Christmas Market) in

December throughout the city, including on Unter den Linden and Alexanderplatz
•**New Year's Eve Celebration**
(Silvester) at the Brandenburg Gate. Fireworks everywhere
•**Six-Day Race** (cycle races) the last week of January (tickets at *www.velomax.de*)

•**Lange Nacht der Museen** (Long Night of the Museums), when most museums are open until 2 a.m. and special events are held; in early February (*www.lange-nacht-der-museen.de*)

•**Berlin International Film Festival** in February (*www.berlinale.de*)

Spring

•**ITB** (a huge international tourism fair) in March (*www.itb-berlin.de*)

•**Theatertreffen Berlin** (Berlin Theater Meeting) in May (*www.berlinerfestspiele.de*)

Summer

•**Karneval der Kulturen** (Carnival of Cultures), parade and festival in early June (*www.karneval-berlin.de*)

•**Christopher Street Day** (gay pride parade), in June (*www.csd-berlin.de*)

•**Fête de la Musique** (world music festival), in June (*www.fetedelamusique.de*)

•**Classic Open Air Berlin** late June/early July, a classical music festival held at Gendarmenmarkt (*www.classicopenair.de*)

•**Loveparade** (techno music fest/counterculture parade), in early July (*www.loveparade.de*)

•**International Beer Festival**, in August (*www.bierfestival-berlin.de*)

•**Lange Nacht der Museen** (Long Night of the Museums), when most museums are open until 2 a.m. and special events are held; in late August (*www.lange-nacht-der-museen.de*)

Autumn

•**Berlin Marathon** late September (*www.berlin-marathon.com*)

•**Art Forum Berlin**, an international fair for contemporary art late September/early October (*www.art-forum-berlin.com*)

•**JazzFest Berlin** in October/November (*www.berlinerfestspiele.de*)

Other Basic Information

Customs

Citizens of the United States who have been away more than 48 hours can bring home $800

of merchandise duty-free every 30 days. For more information, go to Traveler Information ("Know Before You

Go") at *www.customs.gov*. Canadians can bring back C$750 each year if you've been gone for seven days or more.

Doctor

In emergencies, an English-speaking doctor can be reached at Tel. 310031.

Eating

Check out the "Dining" section of this chapter.

Electricity

The electrical current in Germany is 220 volts as opposed to 110 volts found at home. Don't fry your electric razor, hairdryer or laptop. You'll need a converter and an adapter. Some laptops don't require a converter, but why are you bringing one anyway? You're on vacation, remember?

Embassies

U.S. Embassy: *4-5 Neustädtische Kirchstrasse, Tel. 83050*
Canadian Embassy: *95 Friedrichstrasse, Tel. 203120*

E-Mail

Internet cafés seem to pop up everywhere (and go out of business quickly). You shouldn't have difficulty finding a place to e-mail home. The going rate is about €2 per hour. The easyinternetcafe has at least five locations in Berlin, including 224 Kurfürstendamm, 5 Rathausstrasse, and in the Sony Center. They're open 24 hours, seven days a week (and most have Dunkin' Donut shops attached).

Holidays

- January 1: New Year's Day
- Good Friday (movable date)
- Easter and the Monday after Easter (movable date)
- May/Labor Day: May 1
- Ascension Day (40 days after Easter) (movable date)
- Pentecost Monday (movable date)
- Day of German Unity: October 3
- Day of Prayer and Repentance: 3rd Wednesday in November
- December 24: Christmas Eve
- December 25: Christmas
- December 26: Boxing Day

Insurance

Check with your health-care provider. Most policies don't cover you overseas. If that's the case, you may want to obtain medical insurance (one such provider is found at *www.medexassist.com*). Given the uncertainties in today's world, you may also want to purchase trip-cancellation insurance (one provider is *www.travelguard.com*). Make sure that your policy covers sickness, disasters, bankruptcy and State Department travel restrictions and warnings. In other words, read the fine print!

Language

Many younger Germans speak English. This book has a list of helpful German phrases. It's always courteous to learn at least a few of them.

Words in German sometimes look overwhelmingly confusing. They run into each other with none of the helpful spaces we English speakers are used to. For instance, *Tomatencremesuppe* is tomato cream soup. You'll just need to deal with it.

Money

The **euro** (€) is the currency of Germany and most of Europe. Before you leave for Berlin, it's a good idea to get some euros. It makes your arrival a lot easier. Call your credit-card company or bank before you leave to tell them that you'll be using your ATM or credit card outside the country. Many have automatic controls that can "freeze" your account if the computer program determines that there are charges outside your normal area.

ATMs (of course, with fees) are the easiest way to change money in Berlin. You'll find them everywhere, including the airports. They're called "Bankomat" in Germany. You can still get traveler's checks, but why bother?

Museums

Entry to all government-owned museums is free on Thursdays for the last four hours they're open. This includes some of the most popular museums, including Alte Nationalgalerie, Altes Museum, Gemäldegalerie, Neue Nationalgalerie, Pergamonmuseum, and Sammlung Berggruen. You can purchase a *Tageskarte* for €10 at all government-owned museums, allowing entry to as many as you can conquer in a day (excluding special exhibits). You can also purchase one that allows entry for three consecutive days. The *WelcomeCard* is good for two (€16) or three (€22) consecutive days, and provides discounts to certain museums (mostly private museums, including Checkpoint Charlie), tours, and free public transportation within Berlin. You can purchase a *WelcomeCard* at tourist-information centers (listed in this book) and at *www.berlin-tourist-information.de*.

Packing

Never pack prescription drugs, eyeglasses or valuables. Carry them on. Think black. It always works for men and women. Oh, and by the way, pack light. Don't ruin your trip by having to lug around huge suitcases. Before you leave home, make copies of your passport, airline tickets and confirmation of hotel reservations. You should also make a list of your credit-card numbers and the telephone numbers for your credit-card companies. If you lose any of them (or they're stolen), you can call someone at home and have them provide the information to you. You should also pack copies of these documents separate from the originals.

Party Time

Berlin is the only European city that has no official or required closing time for its bars and clubs.

Passports

You'll need a valid passport to enter Germany from the United States and Canada for visits under three months. No visa is required.

Restrooms

There aren't a lot of public restrooms. If you need to go, your best bet is to head (no pun intended) to the nearest café. It's considered good manners to purchase something if you use the restroom. If there's an attendant, tip up to €.50. The city has begun to add coin-operated "City Toilets" in major tourist areas.

Running

Runners and joggers should head to the many paths in the Tiergarten.

Safety

Don't wear a "fanny pack;" it's a sign that you're a tourist and an easy target (especially in crowded tourist areas). Avoid wearing expensive jewelry. The eastern suburbs can be rough, especially for non-Germans.

Shopping

Throughout this guide, you'll find recommended places to shop. Shopping hours in Berlin are highly regulated. From Monday to Friday, shops are allowed to be open between 9 a.m. and 8:30 p.m., and on Saturdays between 9 a.m. and 4 p.m. Most shops are closed on Sundays.

Taxes

Hotel and restaurant prices are required by law to include

taxes and service charges. Value Added Tax is approximately 13% to 20% (higher on luxury goods). The VAT is included in the price of goods. Foreigners are entitled to a refund, but must fill out a refund form. When you make your purchase, you should ask for the form and instructions. There's a refund office at the airport. Yes, it can be a hassle. Check *www.globalrefund.com* for the latest information on refunds (and help for a fee).

Telephone
•Country code for Germany: 49
•Area code for Berlin: 030
•Calling Berlin from the United States and Canada: Dial 011-49-30 plus the local number (note that you omit the initial 0 in the 030 area code)
•Calling the United States or Canada from Berlin: Dial 00 (wait for the tone), dial 1 plus the area code and seven-digit local number
•Calling Berlin from other towns in Germany: Dial 030 plus the local number
•Calling within Berlin: Dial the local number

There's no standard length of local telephone numbers in Berlin. A local number can have anywhere from four to eight digits. Phone cards purchased in Berlin are the cheapest way to call. U.S.-issued calling cards can be expensive to use from Berlin. You can rent a cell phone for use in the city. One such company is www.cellhire.com.

Time
When it's noon in New York City, it's 6 p.m. in Berlin. For hours of events or schedules, Germans use the 24-hour clock. So 6 a.m. is 06h00, and 1 p.m. is 13h00.

Tipping
For tipping in restaurants, see the "Dining" section of this chapter. It's common to tip taxi drivers up to 10%. If a doorman calls a cab for you, tip 1 to €1.50. Tip coat check €.50 to €1. Bellhops expect €1 per bag.

Water
Tap water is safe in Berlin.

Web Sites
•Author's: *www.eatndrink.com*
•City of Berlin: *www.berlin.de/ English*
•Berlin Tourist Information: *www.berlin-tourist-information.de*
•Germany: *www.cometogermany.com*
•U.S. State Department: *www.travel.state.gov*

Weather

Temperatures dip to freezing in winter. Fall and spring are pleasant. Summer is very pleasant. Average high temperature/low temperature/ days of rain:
- January: 35° (1°C)/26° (-3°C)/16
- February: 39° (3°C) /27° (-2°C)/16
- March: 47° (8°C)/ 33°(0°C)/13
- April: 54°(12°C)/37°(2°C)/ 15
- May: 65°(18°C)/45°(7°C)/ 15
- June: 70° (21°C)/ 53°(11°C)/17
- July: 73°(22°C)/56°(13°C)/ 16
- August: 73°(22°C)/ 55°(12°C)/16
- September: 66°(18°C)/ 50°(10°C)/13
- October: 56°(13°C)/ 42°(5°C)/13
- November: 45°(7°C)/ 35°(1°C)/15
- December: 38°(3°C)/30° (-1°C)/15

Check *www.weather.com* before you leave.

Hotels

Prices for two people in a double room

Expensive (over $200)
Adlon
77 Unter den Linden
Tel. 800/426-3135 (toll free)
Tel. 22610
www.hotel-adlon.de

Brandenburger Hof
14 Eislebener Strasse
Tel. 214050
www.brandenburger-hof.de

Grand Hyatt
2 Marlene-Dietrich-Platz
(Potsdamer Platz)
Tel. 800/233-1234 (toll free)
Tel. 25531234
www.hotel-adlon.de

Kempinski Hotel Bristol
27 Kurfürstendamm
Tel. 800/426-3135 (toll free)
Tel. 884340
www.kempinskiberlin.de

Moderate ($125 to $200)
Hollywood Media Hotel
202 Kurfürstendamm
Tel. 888/872-8356 (toll free)
Tel. 889100
www.hollywood-media-hotel.de

Luisenhof
92 Köpenicker Strasse
Tel. 2462810
www.luisenhof.de

Riehmers Hofgarten
83 Yorckstrasse
Tel. 78098800
www.riehmers-hofgarten.de

Unter den Linden
14 Unter den Linden
Tel. 238110
www.hotel-unter-den-linden.de

Inexpensive (under $125)
Bogota
45 Schlüterstrasse
Tel. 8815001
www.hotelbogota.de

Charlottenburger Hof
14 Stuttgarter Platz
Tel. 329070
www.charlottenburger-hof.com

Pension Kastanienhof
65 Kastanienallee
Tel. 443050
www.hotel-kastanienhof-berlin.de

Pension Nürnberger Eck
24A Nürnberger Strasse
Tel. 2351780
www.nuernberger-eck.de

There are also many apartments for rent on the internet.

Helpful Phrases

please, Bitte (*bit-teh*)
thank you, Danke (*dahng-keh*)
yes, Ja (*yah*)
no, Nein (*nine*)
good day/hello, Guten Tag (*goo-tehn tahg*) (between 10am-6pm)
good morning, Guten Morgen (*goo-tehn mor-gen*) (until 10am)
good evening, Guten Abend (*goo-tehn ahb'nt*) (after 6pm)

goodbye, Auf Wiedersehen. (*owf-vee-der-zayn*)
I am sorry, Es tut mir leid. (*es toot meer lite*)
Do you speak English?, Sprechen Sie Englisch? (*shprehkh-ehn zee ehng-lish*)
Excuse me, Entschuldigung. (*ehnt-shool-dig-oong*)
I don't understand, Ich verstehe nicht. (*ikh fehr-shtay-heh nikht*)
help, Hilfe (*hilf-uh*)

Where is…?, Wo ist…? (*voh ist*)

the toilet, die Toilette (*dee toh-leh-teh*)

airport, Flughafen (*floog-hafen*)

train station, Bahnhof (*bahn-hof*)

I'd like…, Ich hätte gern… (*ikh heh-teh gehrn*)

the bill, die Rechnung (*dee rekh-noong*)

a room, ein Zimmer (*eyen tsim-er*)

a ticket, eine Karte (*eye-nuh cart-uh*)

a table, einen Tisch (*eye-nuhn tish*)

a reservation, eine Reservierung (*eye-nuh reh-zer-feer-oong*)

for, für (*fewr*)

one, eins (*eyens*)

two, zwei (*tsvy*)

three, drei, (*dry*)

four, vier (*fear*)

five, fünf (*fewnf*)

six, sechs (*zex*)

seven, sieben (*zee-behn*)

eight, acht (*ahkht*)

nine, neun (*noyn*)

ten, zehn (*tsane*)

left, links (*links*)

right, rechts (*rehkhts*)

today, heute (*hoy-teh*)

tomorrow, morgen (*mor-gehn*)

no smoking, Nichtrauchen (*nikht-rowkh-er*)

what, was (*vahss*)

when, wann (*vunn*)

how, wie (*vee*)

who, wer (*vair*)

this, dies (*deez*)

that, das (*dahs*)

a mistake (error), ein Fehler (*ein fayler*)

service included, mit Bedienung (*mit beh-dee-noong*)

credit card, Kreditkarte (*kreh-deet-kar-teh*)

How much does it cost?, Was kostet das? (*voss kos't duss*)

Is it free?, Ist es umsonst? (*ist ehs oom-zohnst*)

I did not order this, Das habe ich nicht bestellt. (*dahs hah-buh ikh nikht buh-shtelt*)

This is…, Dies ist… (*deez ist*)

too, zu (*tsoo*)

cold, kalt (*kahlt*)

undercooked, nicht lange genug gekocht (*nikht lahng-uh guh-nook geh-kokht*)

overcooked, zu lang gebraten (*tsoo lahng geh-kokht*)

delicious, lecker (*lehk-er*)

I am a…, Ich bin… (*ikh bin*)

vegetarian, Vegetarier (*veh-geh-tar-ee-er*)

diabetic, Diabetiker (*dee-ah-bet-i-ker*)

diet, Diät (*dee-ate*)

I cannot eat…, Ich darf kein…essen. (*ikh darf kine … es-sen*)

meat, Fleisch (*fleyesh*)
pork, Schweinefleisch (*shveye-neh-fleyesh*)
sugar, Zucker (*tsoo-ker*)

open, geöffnet (*geh-urf-neht*)
closed, geschlossen (*geh-shloh-sehn*)
free, frei (*fry*)

men, Herren (*hehr-rehn*)
women, Damen (*dah-mehn*)
Mr., Herr (*hair*)
Mrs., Frau (*frau*)
Miss, Fräulein (*froy-line*)

waiter, Kellner (*kel-ner*)
waitress, Kellnerin (*kel-ner-in*)

Monday, Montag (*moan-tahk*)
Tuesday, Dienstag (*deens-tahk*)
Wednesday, Mittwoch (*mit-voah*)
Thursday, Donnerstag (*doe-ners-tahk*)
Friday, Freitag (*fry-tahk*)
Saturday, Sonnabend/Samstag (*zonn-a-bent/zahm-stakh*)
Sunday, Sonntag (*zone-tahk*)

INDEX

ADLON HOTEL 11, 81
Ägyptisches Museum 24
airports 108
Alexanderplatz/Alexander Square 8, 27, 28, 94
Allied Museum/Alliierten Museum 70
Alte Bibliothek 15
Alte Nationalgalerie 25, 92
Alter St. Matthäus-Kirchhof 58
Altes Museum 24, 92
Ampelmännchen 90
Antik & Flohmarkt/Antique and Flea Market 17
antiques 17
aquarium 29, 52, 93, 95
archeology museum 24
architecture 43, 54, 64
arrival 108
Art Deco 19, 48, 67, 100
art galleries 22
Art Library 47
Art Nouveau 35, 48, 67, 100
arts and crafts museum 48

BAHNHOF FRIEDRICH-STRASSE 16
Bauhaus Museum of Design/ Bauhaus-Archiv 64
beach 72
Bebel Square/Bebelplatz 15, 91
beer festival 112
beer garden/beer hall 51, 62, 67, 102
Berggruen Collection: Picasso and His Era 68, 100
Berlin Airlift 58
Berlin Cathedral 25, 92
Berlin City Hall 29, 93
Berlin Wall 22, 26, 32, 40, 53, 60, 79, 81, 82, 83, 84, 88
Berliner Dom 25, 92
Berliner Mauer 26

Berliner Rathaus 29, 93
bike rentals 111
boat museum 31
Bode Museum/Bodemuseum 24, 92
book market 15, 90
book burning 15, 91
Botanical Garden/Botanischer Garten 72
Brandenburg Gate/Brandenburger Tor 8, 10, 79, 81, 88
Bridge Museum, The 70
Bröhan Museum 67, 100
Brücke-Museum 70
Bundeskanzleramt 53
Bundesministerium der Finanzen 23, 83
Bundespräsidialamt 51, 98
bus tour 110
Byzantine art 24

CANADIAN EMBASSY 113
cars and driving 109
casino 45
cemeteries 39, 58
Chamber Music Hall 47
Chamisso Square/Chamissoplatz 56
Charlottenburg Palace and Gardens 65, 67, 102
Checkpoint Charlie 8, 22, 70, 84
children 29, 32
china and porcelain collection 65
chocolates 21, 62, 84
Christmas market 111
Coin Cabinet 24
Comic Opera Berlin 13, 90
commercial art 47
communist-era architecture 27, 42
communist-era art 23
concentration camp 73
Concert House 20, 86

concerts 25, 49, 112
contemporary art 14, 22, 34, 45, 48, 112
Crown Prince's Palace 91
Crystal Night 34, 73
Cultural Brewery 39
Cultural Forum 46
customs 112
cycling 43, 111

DAHLEM MUSEUM COMPLEX/DAHLEMER MUSEEN 69
DaimlerChrylser Collection 45
Das Verborgene Museum 68
Denkmal für die Ermordeten Juden Europas 8, 17, 81
department stores
  Galeries Lafayette 19, 86
  KaDeWe 63, 95
  Kaufhof 28
  Quartier 206 19, 86
  Wertheim 62
Deutsche Guggenheim Berlin 14, 90
Deutsche Oper Berlin 68
Deutsche Staatsoper 15, 91
Deutscher Dom 20, 21, 86
Deutsches Historisches Museum 16, 92
Deutsches Technikmuseum Berlin 54
dining 104, 105
doctor 113
Dokumentationszentrum Berliner Mauer 32
Drawing and Print Collection 47

EAST SIDE GALLERY 40
eating 104, 105
Egyptian Museum 24, 25
electricity 113
E-Mail 113
embassies 11, 113
Ephraim-Palais 30, 88
Erotic Museum/Erotikmuseum 63
Ethnologisches Museum 69
Expressionism 70
euro 114

Europa-Center/Europe Center 63, 95

FAR EAST ART 69
Federal Chancellery 53
Fernsehturm 28, 93
festivals 111, 112
film festival 112
Film Museum Berlin/ Filmmuseum Berlin 43, 45, 82
flea market 51
food hall 63, 95
foreign phrases 118, 119
Forst Grunewald 69, 71, 72
fountains 28, 29, 42, 93, 94
Franciscan Cloister Church/ Franziskaner Klosterkirche 31
Französischer Dom 20, 86
Frederick the Great 15, 65, 90, 102
French Cathedral 20, 86
French Embassy 11
Friedrichshain 40
Friedrichstrasse Train Station 16
Friedrichswerder Church/ Friedrichswerdersche-Kirche 19, 87
Führerbunker (Hitler's Bunker) 82
Funkturm 68

GARDENS (also see parks) 72, 77
gay/lesbian 54, 57, 112
GDR (German Democratic Republic) 13
Gedenkstätte Deutscher Widerstand 49
Gedenkstätte Grosse Hamburger Strasse 36
Gemäldegalerie 46, 83
Gendarmenmarkt 8, 20, 86
German Cathedral 20, 21, 86
German Finance Ministry 23, 83
German Guggenheim Museum 14, 90
German History Museum 16, 92
German Museum of Technology 54
German Opera Berlin 68

German phrases 118, 119
German Resistance Memorial 49
German State Opera 15, 91
Gestapo 23
ghost subway 13
Glockenturm 71
Grosse Hamburger Strasse Jewish Memorial 36
Grunewald Forest 69, 71, 72
Guggenheim Museum 14, 90

HACKESCHEN HÖFE 35
Hamburg Station Museum of Contemporary Art/Hamburger Bahnhof Museum für Gegenwart 34
Hanf Museum 31
Hansa Quarter/Hansaviertel 53
Haus am Checkpoint Charlie 8, 22, 84
Haus der Kulturen der Welt 52, 99
Haus der Wannsee-Konferenz 72
Heckmann Courtyards/ Heckmannhöfe 35
Helmut Newton Foundation/ Helmut Newton Stiftung 64
Hemp Museum 31
Hidden Museum 68
Historical Harbor Berlin/ Historischer Hafen Berlin 31
Hitler, Adolph 11, 23, 49, 53, 70, 82
Hitler's Bunker 82
holidays 113
Holocaust Memorial 8, 17, 81
Homosexual Museum 56, 57
hotels 117, 118
House of the Wannsee Conference 72
House of World Cultures 52, 99
Hugenottenmuseum 20, 86
Humboldt Universität zu Berlin/ Humboldt University of Berlin 14, 90
Huth Wine House 45

INDIAN ART 69
industrial design museum 39
insurance 113

International Conference Center (ICC) 69
Internet cafés 113

JAZZ 112
Jewish Museum 54
jewish sights 34, 36, 37, 39, 54, 72, 73, 81
Jüdischer Friedhof 39
Jüdisches Museum Berlin 54

KAUFHAUS DES WESTENS (KaDeWe) 63, 95
Kaiser Wilhelm Memorial Church/Kaiser-Wilhelm Gedächtniskirche 8, 63, 94
Kammermusiksaal 47
Karl Marx Avenue/Karl-Marx-Allee 42
Käthe-Kollwitz Museum 62
Kennedy, John F. 58
Knoblauch-Haus 30, 88
Komische Oper Berlin 13, 90
Konzerthaus 20, 86
Kreuzberg 54
Kristallnacht 34, 39, 73
Kronprinzenpalais 91
Kulturbrauerei 39
Kulturforum 8, 46, 83
Kunstbibliothek 47
Kunstgewerbemuseum 48, 83
Kunstsalon 14, 90
Kupferstichkabinett 47
Kurfürstendamm 8, 60, 94

LANDWEHRKANAL 51, 95
language 114, 118, 119, 120

MARATHON 112
Marienkirche 29, 93
markets 16, 23, 56, 59, 111
Märkisches Museum 31
Martin Gropius Building/Martin-Gropius-Bau 49, 83
Marx-Engels-Forum 31, 93
mealtimes 106
Memorial to the Murdered European Jews 8, 17, 81
menu translator 107
modern art 14, 22, 34, 45, 48, 112

Molecule Man 42, 71
money 114
Museum Blind Workshop Otto
    Weidt/Museum
    Blindenwerkstatt Otto Weidt
    36
Museum Europäischer Kulturen
    70
Museum for Communication 21
Museum für Indische Kunst 69
Museum für Islamische Kunst 24
Museum für Kommunikation 21
Museum für Naturkunde 34
Museum für Fotografie 64
Museum für Vor- und
    Frühgeschichte 67, 102
Museum Island 8, 23, 87, 92
Museum Kindheit & Jugend 32
Museum of Arts and Crafts 48,
    83
Museum of Childhood and Youth
    32
Museum of Ethnology 69
Museum of European Cultures 70
Museum of Far East Art 69
Museum of Indian Art 69
Museum of Islamic Art 24
Museum of Photography 64
Museum of Primeval and Early
    History 67, 102
museums (general information)
    114
Museumsinsel 8, 23, 87, 92
Musical Instrument Museum/
    Musikinstrumenten-Museum
    47, 83
Natural History Museum 34

NEUE NATIONALGALERIE
    48, 83
Neue Synagoge 34
Neue Wache 16, 91
Neues Museum 25, 92
New Guard House 16, 91
New Museum 25, 92
New National Gallery 48, 83
New Synagogue 34
Nicholas Quarter 30, 87
Nikolaikirche 30, 88
Nikolaiviertel 30, 87

OBERBAUMBRÜCKE 40
Old Library 15
Old Museum 24, 92
Old National Gallery 25, 92
Old St. Matthew's Churchyard 58
Olympiastadion/Olympic Stadium
    70, 71
opera 13, 15, 68, 91

PACKING 115
Palace of Tears 17
Palace of the Republic/Palast der
    Republik 26, 87, 93
pandas, giant 52
Pariser Platz 11, 79
parks 42, 49, 56, 71, 72, 75, 76,
    77
Parliament Building 8, 52, 53, 99
party time 115
passports 115
Pei, IM 16, 92
Pergamonmuseum 8, 24, 92
Philharmonic Hall/Philharmonie
    47, 83
photography 64
Picasso 68, 100
Picture Gallery 46, 83
Pink Village 57
planetarium 40
police, secret 21
porcelain and china collection 65
postal museum 21
Potsdam 74-78
Potsdamer Platz/Potsdam Square
    8, 43, 82
Prenzlauer Berg 37
public transportation 109, 110

RADIO TOWER 68
Raum der Stille 10, 81
Reichstag 8, 52, 53, 99
restaurant prices 107
restaurants
    Abendmahl 59
    Bierhaus Luisen-Bräu 67, 102
    Borchardt 20
    Café und Restaurant
        Drachenhaus 76
    Café/Bar Viktoria 98
    Carib 57
    Diekmann 45

Dietrich's 46
First Floor 52
Gugelhof 40
Hackescher Hof 35
Il Casolare 59
Ku'damm 195 60
Lorenz Adlon 11
Mar y Sol 68
Marjellchen 64
More 57
Mutter Hoppe 30
Opernpalais/Operncafé 15, 91
QBA 35
Rocco 37
Schleusenkrug 51
Sophieneck 36
Tele-Café 28
Trattoria Paparazzi 40
VAU 20
Wintergarten: Café im
   Literaturhaus 60
Zur Letzten 30
Zur Nolle 16
restaurants, ethnic 56
restrooms 115
Room of Silence 10, 81
Rosenthaler Platz/Rosenthaler
   Square 37
running/jogging 115
Russian Embassy/Russische
   Botschaft 13, 88
Rykestrasse Synagogue 39

SACHSENHAUSEN MUSEUM/
   CONCENTRATION CAMP
   73
safety 115
Sammlung Berggruen: Picasso und
   seine Zeit 68, 100
Sammlung DaimlerChrysler 45
Sans Souci 75, 76, 77
S-Bahn 109
Scandinavian Embassies Complex
   95
Scheunenviertel 32
Schinkel-Museum 19, 87
Schloss Bellevue 8, 51, 98
Schloss Charlottenburg 65, 102
Schlossgarten Charlottenburg 67,
   102

Schlossstrasse Villas 100
Schöneberg 54
Schwules Museum 56, 57
sculpture 24, 25, 71, 100
Sealife Berlin 29, 93
shopping 115
shopping areas 8, 19, 30, 35, 37,
   43, 56, 60, 84, 85
Siegessäule 8, 51, 81, 98
Sony Center 43, 82
Sophien Church/Sophienkirche
   36
souvenirs 35, 52, 56
Soviet War Memorial/Sowjetisches
   Ehrenmal 51, 71
Spandau Citadel 72
Spielbank Berlin 45
St. Hedwigs Cathedral 17, 87
St. Mary's Church 29, 93
St. Matthew's Church 48
St. Nicholas Church 30, 88
Staatsbibliothek 14, 48, 83, 90
Stasi-Die Ausstellung/Stasi-The
   Exhibit 21
State Library 14, 48, 83, 90
St. Hedwigs-Kathedrale 17, 87
St. Matthäus-Kirche 48
Story of Berlin 60
Synagoge Rykestrasse 39
synagogues 34, 39

TAXES 115
technology museum 54
telephones 116
Television Tower 8, 28, 93
theaters 13, 35, 43, 63, 82, 90,
   95, 112
Tiergarten 8, 49, 82, 98
time 116
tipping 106, 116
Topographie des Terrors/
   Topography of Terror 22, 83
tourist-information centers 10,
   28, 63
Tränenpalast 17
Treptower Park 71
Trödelmarkt 51
Türkenmarkt/Turkish Market 59

U-BAHN 109
U.S. Embassy 11, 81, 113

unknown concentration camp
    victims 16, 91
unknown soldier 16, 91
Unter den Linden 8, 11, 13, 88

VEGETARIAN 59
Velodrom 43
Victory Column 8, 51, 81, 98
views 25, 28, 29, 51, 63, 71, 93,
    98
Viktoriapark 56

WALKS
    Berlin Wall 79
    Charottenburg 100
    East Berlin 88

Gendarmenmarkt 84
    West Berlin 94
Wasserturm 37
water 106, 116
Water Tower 37
weather 117
web sites 116
Weinhaus Huth 45
WelcomeCard 110, 114
women artists 68

ZEISS PLANETARIUM/ZEISS-
    GROSSPLANETARIUM 40
Zitadelle Spandauer 72
Zoo/Zoologischer Garten Berlin
    8, 52, 95

Made Easy Guides

The World's Best Sights & Walks–Made Easy!

Amsterdam

Berlin

London

Paris

Provence & the

French Riviera

Rome

Florence

Venice

Dublin

Europe

New York City